Education as Humanisation

Over the past decades, the ambiguity with regard to the role of education in the context of post-conflict and divided societies has consistently maintained its poignancy for scholars and practitioners. Most recently, global developments, including the after-effects of the Arab Spring, the devastating wars in Syria and the refugee crisis in Europe, have directed our attention once more to the part that education can play in building peace at many levels.

Therefore, it is timely to create a space for a focused inquiry and scholarly debate about what may constitute peace-oriented pedagogies and how they might affect the post-conflict reconstruction in divergent settings. Both the subject and the contents of this book are important especially in the light of the current needs in many societies emerging from conflicted community relations. They provide a refreshing and transformative view of peace based on a humanising conception of education and dialogic pedagogy.

With its thought-provoking philosophical investigations and rich empirical inquiries, the book strives to engage readers in re-examining some of the key concepts in peace-building education and in identifying pivotal underlying issues in the field. Furthermore, by offering a principled, persuasive conceptual framework and by problematising implementations and interventions in practice, it can serve to provoke more evaluations and constructive critiques of education as humanisation and dialogic pedagogy. Thus the book will appeal to peace educators, educational thinkers, peace researchers, practitioners, policy-makers, NGO workers and the public.

This book was originally published as a special issue of *Compare: A Journal of Comparative and International Education*.

Scherto Gill is a Research Fellow at the Guerrand-Hermès Foundation for Peace, Brighton, UK, and Visiting Research Fellow at the University of Sussex, Brighton, UK. She writes in the fields of education, peace and dialogue, her most recent publications include *Rethinking Secondary Education* (2013), *Religion, Spirituality and Human Flourishing* (2014) and *Why Love Matters: Values in Governance* (2015).

Ulrike Niens has worked as a Researcher and Senior Lecturer at Ulster University, Coleraine, Northern Ireland, and Queen's University Belfast, Northern Ireland. Her research and teaching focused on education for peace and democracy in divided societies. She was a member of the editorial and the international editorial board of *Compare* from 2009–2014. She is currently taking a career break and is working as a Clinical Psychologist in Germany.

Education as Humanisation
Dialogic pedagogy in post-conflict peacebuilding

Edited by
Scherto Gill and Ulrike Niens

LONDON AND NEW YORK

First published 2016
by Routledge
2 Park Square, Milton Park, Abingdon, Oxon, OX14 4RN, UK

and by Routledge
711 Third Avenue, New York, NY 10017, USA

Routledge is an imprint of the Taylor & Francis Group, an informa business

© 2016 British Association for International and Comparative Education

All rights reserved. No part of this book may be reprinted or reproduced or utilised in any form or by any electronic, mechanical, or other means, now known or hereafter invented, including photocopying and recording, or in any information storage or retrieval system, without permission in writing from the publishers.

Trademark notice: Product or corporate names may be trademarks or registered trademarks, and are used only for identification and explanation without intent to infringe.

British Library Cataloguing in Publication Data
A catalogue record for this book is available from the British Library

ISBN 13: 978-1-138-64636-0

Typeset in Times New Roman
by RefineCatch Limited, Bungay, Suffolk

Publisher's Note
The publisher accepts responsibility for any inconsistencies that may have arisen during the conversion of this book from journal articles to book chapters, namely the possible inclusion of journal terminology.

Disclaimer
Every effort has been made to contact copyright holders for their permission to reprint material in this book. The publishers would be grateful to hear from any copyright holder who is not here acknowledged and will undertake to rectify any errors or omissions in future editions of this book.

Contents

Citation Information vii
Notes on Contributors ix

Introduction – Education as humanisation: dialogic pedagogy in post-conflict peacebuilding 1
Scherto Gill and Ulrike Niens

1. Education as humanisation: a theoretical review on the role of dialogic pedagogy in peacebuilding education 10
Scherto Gill and Ulrike Niens

2. Contextual and pedagogical considerations in teaching for forgiveness in the Arab world 32
Ilham Nasser, Mohammed Abu-Nimer and Ola Mahmoud

3. Global citizenship as education for peacebuilding in a divided society: structural and contextual constraints on the development of critical dialogic discourse in schools 53
Jacqueline Reilly and Ulrike Niens

4. Articulating injustice: an exploration of young people's experiences of participation in a conflict transformation programme that utilises the arts as a form of dialogue 77
Heather Knight

5. Lebanese youth narratives: a bleak post-war landscape 97
Roseanne Saad Khalaf

6. Reconciliation through dialogical nostalgia in post-conflict societies: a curriculum to intersect 117
Petro du Preez

Index 137

Citation Information

The chapters in this book were originally published in *Compare: A Journal of Comparative and International Education*, volume 44, issue 1 (January 2014). When citing this material, please use the original page numbering for each article, as follows:

Editorial
Education as humanisation: dialogic pedagogy in post-conflict peacebuilding
Scherto Gill and Ulrike Niens
Compare: A Journal of Comparative and International Education, volume 44, issue 1 (January 2014) pp. 1–9

Chapter 1
Education as humanisation: a theoretical review on the role of dialogic pedagogy in peacebuilding education
Scherto Gill and Ulrike Niens
Compare: A Journal of Comparative and International Education, volume 44, issue 1 (January 2014) pp. 10–31

Chapter 2
Contextual and pedagogical considerations in teaching for forgiveness in the Arab world
Ilham Nasser, Mohammed Abu-Nimer and Ola Mahmoud
Compare: A Journal of Comparative and International Education, volume 44, issue 1 (January 2014) pp. 32–52

Chapter 3
Global citizenship as education for peacebuilding in a divided society: structural and contextual constraints on the development of critical dialogic discourse in schools
Jacqueline Reilly and Ulrike Niens
Compare: A Journal of Comparative and International Education, volume 44, issue 1 (January 2014) pp. 53–76

CITATION INFORMATION

Chapter 4
Articulating injustice: an exploration of young people's experiences of participation in a conflict transformation programme that utilises the arts as a form of dialogue
Heather Knight
Compare: A Journal of Comparative and International Education, volume 44, issue 1 (January 2014) pp. 77–96

Chapter 5
Lebanese youth narratives: a bleak post-war landscape
Roseanne Saad Khalaf
Compare: A Journal of Comparative and International Education, volume 44, issue 1 (January 2014) pp. 97–116

Chapter 6
Reconciliation through dialogical nostalgia in post-conflict societies: a curriculum to intersect
Petro du Preez
Compare: A Journal of Comparative and International Education, volume 44, issue 1 (January 2014) pp. 117–135

For any permission-related enquiries please visit:
http://www.tandfonline.com/page/help/permissions

Notes on Contributors

Mohammed Abu-Nimer is a Professor in the School of International Service and Director of the Peacebuilding and Development Institute at American University, Washington D.C., USA. He has conducted interreligious conflict resolution training and interfaith dialogue workshops in conflict areas around the world. He is the co-founder and co-editor of the *Journal of Peacebuilding and Development*.

Petro du Preez is Professor of Curriculum Studies at the North West University, Potchefstroom, South Africa. Her research is in the areas of curriculum studies for diverse religious and cultural contexts, human rights education for social transformation and research methodology. She has published widely, presented international papers and promoted several studies on these topics.

Scherto Gill is a Research Fellow at the Guerrand-Hermès Foundation for Peace, Brighton, UK, and Visiting Research Fellow at the University of Sussex, Brighton, UK. She writes in the fields of education, peace and dialogue, her most recent publications include *Rethinking Secondary Education* (2013), *Religion, Spirituality and Human Flourishing* (2014) and *Why Love Matters: Values in Governance* (2015).

Roseanne Saad Khalaf is Associate Professor of English and Creative Writing at the American University of Beirut, Lebanon. She is the author and editor of eight books, among them: *Transit Beirut* (2003); *Hikayat: Short Stories by Lebanese Women* (2006); and most recently, *Arab Society and Culture* (2009) and *Arab Youth: Social Mobilization in Times of Risk* (2011), both co-edited with Samir Khalaf. Currently, she is conducting a narrative study on the views of Arab youth.

Heather Knight is Associate Lecturer in Education Studies at the University of Plymouth, UK, where she is currently completing her PhD. Her research explores the role of the arts for teaching and learning about issues of racism, racial conflict and diversity in predominantly 'white' areas.

Ola Mahmoud is a Research Officer with the Center for Academic Mobility Research at the Institute of International Education, New York City, NY, USA. She manages Project Atlas, a collaborative global initiative that collects and disseminates current data on higher education mobility trends of students worldwide. She also conducts research for IIE's Generation Study Abroad.

NOTES ON CONTRIBUTORS

Ilham Nasser is Associate Professor of Early Childhood Education at George Mason University, Fairfax, VA, USA. She has researched and published on the topic of teacher development including teachers' motivation, teacher preparation, and professional development and teaching for peace, with a focus on foreign language teaching and bilingual education as a means to promote peace education in early childhood settings. She is the editor of *Examining Education, Media, and Dialogue under Occupation* (with Lawrence Berlin and Shelly Wong, 2011).

Ulrike Niens has worked as a Researcher and Senior Lecturer at Ulster University, Coleraine, Northern Ireland, and Queen's University Belfast, Northern Ireland. Her research and teaching focused on education for peace and democracy in divided societies. She was a member of the editorial and the international editorial board of *Compare* from 2009–2014. She is currently taking a career break and is working as a Clinical Psychologist in Germany.

Jacqueline Reilly is Senior Lecturer in Education at the Institute for Research in Social Sciences at the University of Ulster, Coleraine, Northern Ireland, where she is Head of the Research Graduate School in the Faculty of Social Sciences. Her research interests lie broadly within the area of education for social justice and encompass education for local and global citizenship, human rights education and training, and peace education, particularly with a focus on issues of identity and divided societies.

INTRODUCTION

Education as humanisation: dialogic pedagogy in post-conflict peacebuilding

In the context of post-conflict and divided societies working towards building peace, it has been widely recognised that education can play a critical part in either fermenting community division or in assisting socio-political change leading to the reconstruction of community relationships. Over the past decades, the ambiguity with regard to the role of education in such contexts has consistently attracted the attention of and maintained its poignancy for academics, educational policy makers and practitioners as well as the public. This has been reflected in a number of articles and special issues published in *Compare* since the journal was established, with one of its first issues focusing on the debate about 'Diversity and Unity in Education' (Boucher 1978). The issue of education for conflict or for peace has since featured in articles from around the world and after the September 11 terrorist attacks in New York, concerns about the role of education in such contexts resurged globally, which was echoed in a Special Issue, 'Education in the Twenty-First Century: Conflict, Reconciliation and Reconstruction', in 2005 (Leach 2005).

Most recently, global developments, including the after-effects of the Arab Spring, the devastating conflict in Syria and international withdrawal from countries like Afghanistan and Iraq, have directed our attention once more to the consequences of ethno-political conflict and its influence at many levels. A central question to be posed, then, is how to conceptualise, develop and refine pedagogical strategies in post-conflict societies to ensure that education proactively and constructively supports sustainable peacebuilding.

In this context, we believe that it is vital to create a space for initiating a focused inquiry and scholarly debate about peacebuilding pedagogies and how they might affect the post-conflict reconstruction in divergent socio-political, cultural, geographical and educational settings.

Both the subject and the content of this Special Issue, 'Education as Humanisation: Dialogic Pedagogy in Post-Conflict Peacebuilding', are timely in light of the current needs in many divided societies emerging from conflicted community relations. Reinstating humanisation as both the aim and process of education in post-conflict peacebuilding is a compelling vision at present, especially when the role of education is perceived as controversial and the pressure for economic growth and recovery tends to drive education towards a more impoverished model. We believe that promoting dialogic pedagogy can help to ensure that individuals and communities can become more aware of those beliefs and practices that perpetuate a system of control, oppression and dehumanisation in order to transform them.

Thus, this Special Issue will help educational thinkers, researchers, practitioners, policy-makers and non-governmental organisation workers re-examine some of the key concepts in peacebuilding education and identify hopeful approaches and pedagogic strategies, especially in terms of how they may present new ways to meet global, regional and national challenges relating to societal divisions.

Education as humanisation and dialogic pedagogy in peacebuilding

In this Special Issue, the notion of humanisation allows us to draw our attention to two pressing agendas in peacebuilding education.

On the one hand, humanisation presents an important opportunity to focus our understanding of peacebuilding as a transformative process, at the core of which lies the effort to restore and repair the interrupted relationships between peoples and communities. This conception of peacebuilding places hope on people's willingness, commitment and determination to (re) connect with each other at the level of our common humanity.

Indeed, in post-conflict and divided societies, there is no standardised formula for peacebuilding, although there is some consensus that strategies such as restoring justice, nation-building and political reforms have to form a key part of it (Lederach 1997). Despite the end of violent conflict, some of these societies continue to be riven with grievances, animosity, fear and the brutalising effects of group stereotyping, amongst other things. This has been argued to be partly due to the fact that people remain living in the shadow of collective memories about trauma from a violent past, which reinforce community divisions (Staub et al. 2005). Individuals may not be aware that the fundamental beliefs and perceptions underpinning the views they are holding against the 'Other' may continue to serve as a major source of disharmony. Thus, an emphasis on tackling the human element of contemporary conflicts by addressing such underlying assumptions and thereby, hopefully, radically restructuring social relations, can further support traditional peacebuilding strategies mentioned above.

In this way, identifying and addressing the roots of conflict and violence that often reside in the personal and collective attitudes towards the Other is, in effect, active humanisation, which can help individuals and groups to become more open-minded and more accepting of the Other. It is within a common humanity that empathy and compassion can transcend animosity, fear and hostility towards the Other and, as a result, open the possibility for forgiveness and reconciliation at personal, interpersonal and intergroup levels. Therefore, humanisation could be argued to be at the core of developing solidarity and social cohesion in post-conflict societies.

On the other hand, humanisation affirms the aim of education as centred on the notion of learning as the process of becoming more fully human, which Freire ([1970] 1996, 37) argues to be the individual's 'ontological and historical vocation'. Humanising education can cultivate in learners a set of values and approaches that have the potential of enabling members of a given community to reengage with the Other, and restore relationships, thereby contributing to healing the wounds left by the traumatic pasts and making an unconditional commitment to sustainable peace.

As the articles in this Special Issue illustrate, this explicit aspiration for humanisation must be co-intentional, where the teachers and students strive to engage in critical thinking and inquiry in a 'quest for mutual humanisation' (Freire [1970] 1996, 56). In such a critical process, the educator and the educatee work together to reflect on 'the very condition of existence … [and] discover each other to be "in a situation"' (90). In other words, '[t]o exist, humanly, is to name the world, to change it' (69). In this way, humanising education not only aims to help the learners identify settings and circumstances in society that may be dehumanising, but also equips them to individually or collectively challenge such situations in order to transform them.

In this Special Issue, the transformative view of peace and the humanising conception of education are accompanied by an argument that dialogic pedagogy is a key avenue for post-conflict peacebuilding. This argument is supported by Wegerif's (2013) recognition of the reciprocal relationship between 'education *for* dialogue' and 'education *through* dialogue' as he claims that, 'dialogue is not only treated as a means to an end but also treated as an end in itself' (33). This is a reflection of what Gadamer (1976) highlighted as the 'dialogue that we are' (as cited in Cesare 2007, 158). Thus, the precondition for true humanisation, Freire [1970] 1996) argued, is dialogue that consists of both reflection and action, or praxis. The development of praxis, or theory and practice in dialogue, must be carried out in horizontal collaboration between the educator and the educatee and be characterised by mutual trust and even love for life and for the world and faith in humanity. It can thus be argued that dialogic pedagogy is humanising education, when implemented effectively, and can help develop individuals' critical awareness of community perspectives, foster mutual understanding and, ultimately, build trust and restore dignity. As this Special Issue elucidates, dialogue, as applied in formal and non-formal education settings, is not seen as limited to discourse, but may also include curriculum activities, biographical (creative) writing, narrative exchange, storytelling, expressive arts and so forth. As such, it may address, to a greater or lesser extent, reflection and/or action, and emphasise, to varying degrees, intra-personal, interpersonal, intragroup or intergroup dialogue.

Whilst scholars and practitioners stress the need for dialogic pedagogy in peacebuilding education, and despite the fact that dialogue has been incorporated in different forms into both formal and non-formal education, little attention has been paid in the theoretical and empirical literature to explore the challenges and limitations that educators face in practice. Additionally, it is seldom explored what methods of dialogue may be most appropriately employed in the divergent cultural and socio-political contexts, the particularities of educational settings as well as educators' experiences. In this regard, the Special Issue explores some of these dynamics in order to unfold the complexities in applying more humanistic approaches to peacebuilding.

The outline of the Special Issue

Indeed, what this Special Issue seeks to highlight and explore is the urgent need for more theoretical development and empirical investigation in terms of how education as humanisation is best conceived and practised through dialogic pedagogy in post-conflict settings.

Placing humanisation and dialogic pedagogies as both the focus and locus of peacebuilding education marks this Special Issue's unique contribution to the field, especially as it sets out to critically examine the normative frameworks that underpin humanisation and dialogic pedagogies in peacebuilding as well as evaluate the potential impact of such approaches in diverse post-conflict areas, for example in Africa, Europe, the Middle East and multicultural societies in general. The articles in this Special Issue also enable the analysis and comparison of theoretical perspectives, teaching and learning practices and policy implications in different educational settings, namely in primary and post-primary schools, higher education and non-formal education. Through such comparative lenses, the Special Issue further recommends directions for more rigorous research approaches in this area.

We start this Special Issue with a conceptual paper, authored by ourselves, that gives an overview, from the perspective of the contemporary literature, of the existing landscape with regard to the role of education in peacebuilding and the pluralistic pedagogical strategies applicable in post-conflict countries. Through such a survey, our paper identifies the notion of humanisation as the concept that unifies most of the existing pedagogical approaches examined in our review. We further argue that peacebuilding education through humanisation can be realised by dialogue and critical reflection, as evidenced in most of the curricular initiatives and pedagogical interventions surveyed. From here, we expand on the notion of humanisation and critical dialogue as a compelling conceptual framework for peacebuilding education.

In the light of this pedagogical framework, the subsequent articles in this Special Issue set out to examine conceptually and to evaluate empirically the role of humanisation and dialogic pedagogies that are aimed at transforming the memories of violence, divisive narratives and dehumanising perceptions of the Other, towards future-shaping discourses of dignity, human relationships and solidarity.

How can we envisage the implementation of humanisation and dialogic pedagogies within schools? Ilham Nasser, Mohammed Abu-Nimer, and Ola Mahmoud argue that this must begin with teachers. In a recent qualitative study with schoolteachers in the Middle East, they examined how such approaches might be understood and implemented in schools through forgiveness education and how the notion of forgiveness as the basis for building a culture of peace may be contextualised in the current socio-political developments in the Arab societies. Here, forgiveness is understood as humanising in that it allows a deeper encounter and empathising with the Other, which forms a part of civics education curriculum in schools. Based on qualitative interviews with teachers in Jordan, Lebanon, Egypt and Palestine, the research findings highlight a complex web of influences that appeared to inform teachers' views on teaching for forgiveness. Whilst religion and history represented important sources that fed into their perspectives, teaching practices were often rooted in less traditional ideas. As such, the interviews indicated a gap in perception of the current social and political realities and the internal religious discourses relating to forgiveness, reconciliation and peacebuilding. Despite such challenges, compounded by a need for further training and resources, the interviewees demonstrated a remarkable level of optimism relating to the potential of teaching forgiveness in the Arab contexts and teachers reported actively incorporating forgiveness, particularly in their citizenship classrooms. The authors of this article conclude that creating spaces for dialogue about forgiveness at an individual and/or school level has to incorporate reflections on wider societal, cultural and religious discourses and may ultimately contribute to individual and societal wellbeing. They further highlight the need for pedagogical guidelines and practical approaches to assist teachers to embark on curriculum interventions in their classrooms.

Continuing the investigation into dialogic pedagogies and discourse in school settings and once again using citizenship education as the main focus, Jacqueline Reilly and Ulrike Niens explore how teachers' understandings of citizenship may be reflected in pupils' views in the context of societal division in Northern Ireland. In contrast to the previous article, the authors here argue that critical reflection and dialogue need to be addressed at the collective level rather than the individual level and relate to controversial societal issues, such as divergent historical narratives as well as current political issues, in order to challenge inequalities and to promote sustainable peace. The qualitative and quantitative research data reported in this study highlight a lack of teacher time and resources as an impediment to dialogue and critical reflection on controversial issues in classroom teaching. The boundaries of the segregated educational systems in Northern

Ireland were interpreted to be reflected in pedagogical strategies as well as in students' perspectives of citizenship, which the authors suggest may reinforce intergroup differentiation rather than promote a shared understanding and common vision of a future society and peace amongst the next generation. It is argued that critical dialogic pedagogies through citizenship education may be limited, especially in relation to their potential to promote positive attitudes and activism that fosters reconciliation and solidarity in Northern Ireland, unless they enable reflective engagement with local and global controversial issues.

Heather Knight takes us beyond classroom settings and addresses dialogue through an examination of informal and extra-curricular activities that are aimed at reconciliation and solidarity. By exploring young people's engagement with the Art: a Resource for Reconciliation Over the World (ARROW) programme in different countries, this research reflects on an educational approach that employs arts as a form of dialogue towards peacebuilding, where the pedagogical focus is placed on rebuilding human relationships. Located within a collaboration of international universities, including those in the UK, South Africa, Palestine, Kosovo and later in other countries, the ARROW programme utilises the arts as a language for sharing stories of conflict, oppression and injustice to promote critical dialogue between academics, practitioners and young people growing up in divided communities. Drawing on focus-group data with the Plymouth ARROW youth group and observational data collected during a week of arts activities between the Plymouth ARROW youth group and the South Africa ARROW youth group, and through arts activities that took place during a UK ARROW congress held in Plymouth, as well as interviews with practitioners, the author contrasts verbal dialogue with arts-based dialogue and proposes that the latter can complement the former through its ability to transcend verbal language barriers, to allow previously silenced narratives to be articulated and to encourage people to think more critically about themselves, humanity and the world. As such, arts-based approaches are argued to address the criticism that dialogue, due to its emphasis on language and voice, which may in themselves privilege the powerful within societies, may fail to tackle structural inequalities including discrimination, social disadvantage and poverty that are often part of the root causes of conflict.

Roseanne Khalaf's article expands on the divergent forms of dialogue through the lenses of personal narratives of young Lebanese university students. It considers creative writing and narrative sharing as a pedagogical approach to critical reflection and action as in Freire's conception. The core of the article is to identify the themes that define the lives of young people in post-war Lebanon, a society that remains divided. An analysis of personal narrative texts that Lebanese students composed over the last 16 years shows an increased sentiment of feeling trapped in between the country's histories of violence, conflicting collective memories and collective amnesia, compounded by a frustration with the present dysfunctional political systems that promise no hope for the future. Khalaf summarises her students' texts under three key themes over time: idealism (1998–2005), activism (2005–2008) and disillusionment (2008–present). As the society struggles to deal with mounting hostility between communities and sectarian rivalries, young Lebanese's aspiration for societal transformation through collective action and democratic participation is replaced by a sense of hopelessness and escape to self-indulgence and gratification. Furthermore, the seemingly never-ending regional conflicts in the Middle East continue to split Lebanese loyalty and alliance and feed sectarian division. In this context, Khalaf concludes that engaging young Lebanese university students in such narrative dialogue can serve to critically challenge structural constraints and disrupt dehumanising and divisive narratives that could possibly perpetuate a cycle of violence.

Through the insights developed in these four empirical studies into perspectives of humanisation and dialogic pedagogy, the Special Issue urges us to re-assess the complexity of education for post-conflict peacebuilding and to take into account a host of contiguous analytical factors when deciding the focus of curriculum and pedagogical interventions, such as cultural discourses, historical narratives and memories, political structure, social policy, religion and more. Thus, the last article of this Special Issue, by Petro du Preez, argues that it is possible to begin framing a peaceful space where competing narratives intersect through dialogue. The author proposes to do so by reconceptualising the notion of nostalgia in new ways. Here, the concept of nostalgia is developed beyond the usual boundaries of sentiment and stagnation, which could be seen as the root of continuing societal division in the context of post-conflict societies. Instead, it is argued that nostalgia should be seen as a narrative nuance with the potential to stimulate dialogue in the context of a curriculum that makes intersections between divergent narratives possible. Seventeen years after the end of apartheid in South Africa, du Preez examines racial segregation and violence in today's South African society, which are still prominent in the verbal and symbolic narrative encounters between people and which demonstrate an overt feeling of nostalgia or longing for (an idealistic) past. In such societies, the author proposes that nostalgia should be seen as an ethical imperative for de-silencing multiple voices about the past and for encouraging reconciliatory discourses in curriculum development. du Preez concludes that our thinking about curricula needs to evolve to respond to the shifting post-conflict social demands in order to keep up with processes of reconciliation.

Conclusion

The articles in this Special Issue highlight the opportunities and challenges of humanising education and dialogic pedagogy for peacebuilding in divergent socio-political and educational contexts. The insights provided through the different perspectives unfolded the often implicit underpinning assumptions of such educational approaches, their challenges and how they may contribute to sustainable peacebuilding in the context of post-conflict and societal divisions.

Despite the influence of theoretical perspectives building on Freire's conceptualisation of humanisation and dialogue in peacebuilding education, empirical research in this area remains relatively scarce. As such, the articles in this Special Issue can only represent a fraction of the actual educational work undertaken in the field. Nevertheless, they stress the contextually bounded nature of the work and clearly demonstrate the need for further developing theories and research in this area. The gap between theory, practice and research has often been identified in the educational literature and is particularly evident in literature concerning peacebuilding education.

Hence this Special Issue – the initial idea for which originated from a thematic session convened by Scherto Gill at the UK Forum for International Education and Training (UKFIET) International Conference on Education and Development held in September 2011 in Oxford – strives to offer a refreshing philosophical conceptualisation of peacebuilding education and, at the same time, engage with a pedagogical framework thus inspired from the practitioners' perspectives. Furthermore, using a number of empirical projects, the Special Issue elicits insights into the relationships between normative assumptions in the field, other theoretical conceptualisations and perspectives, and curriculum and pedagogical interventions and implementations aiming to expound on such theories.

It is certainly the hope of this Special Issue of *Compare* that by identifying some key underlying issues in peacebuilding education, by offering a principled, persuasive conceptual framework and by problematising implementations and interventions in practice, this collection of articles can serve to provoke more appraisals, evaluations and constructive critiques of humanisation and dialogic pedagogy in peacebuilding education.

References

Boucher, L. 1978. "Editorial." *Compare: A Journal of Comparative and International Education* 8 (1): 1–2.
Cesare, D. 2007. *Gadamer, a Philosophical Portrait*. Translated by N. Keane. Bloomington: Indiana University Press.
Freire, P. [1970] 1996. *Pedagogy of the Oppressed*. London: Penguin Books.
Gadamer, H.-G. 1976. *Philosophical Hermeneutics*. Translated and edited by D. Linge. Berkeley, CA: University of California Press.
Leach, F. 2005. "Editorial." *Compare: A Journal of Comparative and International Education* 35 (4): 351–356.
Lederach, J. P. 1997. *Building Peace: Sustainable Reconciliation in Divided Societies*. Washington, DC: United States Institute of Peace Press.

Staub, E., L. A. Pearlman, A. Gubin, and A. Hagengimana. 2005. "Healing, Reconciliation, Forgiving and the Prevention of Violence after Genocide or Mass Killing: An Intervention and Its Experimental Evaluation in Rwanda." *Journal of Social and Clinical Psychology* 24 (3): 297–334.

Wegerif, R. 2013. *Dialogic: Education for the Internet Age*. London: Routledge.

Scherto Gill
Guerrand-Hermès Foundation for Peace, Brighton, UK

Ulrike Niens
Queen's University Belfast, Belfast, UK

Education as humanisation: a theoretical review on the role of dialogic pedagogy in peacebuilding education

Scherto Gill[a] and Ulrike Niens[b]

[a]Centre for Research in Human Development, Guerrand-Hermès Foundation, Brighton, UK; [b]School of Education, Queen's University Belfast, Belfast, UK

In this literature review, we explore the potential role of education in supporting peacebuilding and societal transformation after violent conflict. Following a critical analysis of the literature published by academics and practitioners, we identify the notion of humanisation (as in the seminal works of Paulo Freire and others) as a unifying conceptual core. Peacebuilding education as humanisation is realised by critical reflection and dialogue in most curricular initiatives reviewed, an approach aimed at overcoming the contextual educational constraints often rooted in societal division and segregation, strained community relations and past traumas. We argue that education as humanisation and critical dialogue can offer pedagogical strategies and provide a compelling conceptual framework for peacebuilding education. Such a conceptual framework can serve as a basis for research in the area, especially in contexts where educational institutions tend to be structured to dehumanise.

Introduction

Peacebuilding through education has been identified as one of the major challenges in promoting Millennium Development Goals and building long-term, sustainable peace in post-conflict and divided societies (Oxfam 2008; Save the Children 2008; UNESCO 2011). The importance of education for peacebuilding has been recognised in such societies, as evidenced, for example, by the recent International Decade for a Culture of Peace and Non-violence for the Children of the World (2001–2010), which declared formal and informal education as necessary means to instil in children and young people the knowledge, values, attitudes and skills required for living peacefully together.

However, despite the growing appreciation of the role of education in promoting a culture of peace, there remain an array of ambiguities in terms of our understanding of the key concepts involved. There is also a lack of compelling theories that underpin education for peacebuilding across the academic disciplines. Furthermore, it is increasingly recognised that education ought to play a key and proactive role in creating a culture of peace in schools and communities, yet where there are peace-related programmes in formal and informal educational settings, they are often born out of the need to meet immediate demands for intervention and hence lack in theoretically informed strategies and rigorous evaluation (Bajaj 2004). The situation thus reinforces the oft-lamented disconnection between peacebuilding practice, theory and research (UNICEF 2011).

In this article, we review and analyse key issues in peacebuilding educational initiatives in order to identify a theoretical framework that helps to bridge the above divide. The article first explores literature relating to peacebuilding and the role of education in peacebuilding, followed by an investigation into some of the existing peace-oriented pedagogical practices, especially within post-conflict societies. In doing so, the review identifies a major theoretical underpinning of peacebuilding education, as in Paulo Freire and others' seminal works, on critical dialogue and education as humanisation. We conclude that recognising these ideas and their theoretical contribution to the field is crucial to conducting empirical research that can further develop our understanding of how peacebuilding education can be implemented effectively in divergent socio-political and educational contexts.

Peacebuilding as a transformative process

Peacebuilding is difficult to define as a concept and to achieve in practice (Lambourne 2004; Morris 2000). In order to better understand the concept of peacebuilding for our own purpose, we have chosen not to enter the minefield of contested definitions. Instead, we focus on the literature that conceptualises peacebuilding as a transformative process.

Galtung (1975) introduced the notion of peacebuilding, and distinguished *peacemaking* and *peacekeeping* as the immediate responses to conflict from *peacebuilding* as a means to build a sustainable peaceful future. Peacebuilding thus goes beyond the notion of 'negative peace' (as an absence of war) and involves the development of 'positive peace' characterised by conditions in a society that promote harmony between people, including respect, justice and inclusiveness, as well as 'sustainable peace' that incorporates processes to address the root causes of violent conflict (Galtung 1976).

Similarly, Lederach (1998) stresses the importance of conceptualising peacebuilding as part of the greater process of sustainable social transformation, firmly rooted 'in the relationship of involved parties' (75). In this regard, peacebuilding strategies must stress the centrality of building relationship and relational transformation alongside structural transformation. For Lederach, lasting peace is a creative vision of human society at the heart of which are reframed relationships between people, institutions, social space and natural environment, as well as re-imagined relationships between our past, present and future.

Many authors join Galtung and Lederach in recognising the importance of peacebuilding as a transformative process. Mitchell (2003) considers such transformation as located within structural, personal and relationship changes towards engendering the moral growth of the society. Maiese (2003) advocates a holistic understanding of peacebuilding (materialistic, socio-political, cultural, philosophical, local and international, institutional) that concerns the entire civil society and the individuals within it, that promotes human values and that is future-oriented and hope-inspiring. This holistic view of peacebuilding is based on an understanding of conflict and its root causes, relationship building and reconciliation and how these concepts play out in human society (Lederach 2003, 2005).

Indeed, such conceptualisations of peacebuilding may be seen as idealistic and utopian in their unsubstantiated hope for the potential role of education in promoting long-term sustainable peace. Critics of this view might point out that they may actually hinder the development of realistic strategies to reduce conflict and division, fail to address political and cultural constraints and imbalances and thereby serve to maintain the status quo (Bekerman 2012). However, we would argue that hope and idealism are essential for pedagogical attempts to promote positive human relationships, foster a sense of common humanity and, ultimately, to make the world a better place (Hansen et al. 2009).

The role of education in peacebuilding

It has been proposed that education should be regarded as a critical component of societal transformation after violent conflict (Collier and Hoeffler 2002; Smith and Vaux 2003). Exploring the existing debates, we focus on the role of education in peacebuilding, which incorporates educational strategies aimed at transforming societal divisions and conflict into peaceful and sustainable relationships. This is in line with how UNICEF (2011) defines education for peacebuilding as:

> framed in terms of a development role for education through reforms to the education sector itself and by contributing to political, economic and social transformations in post-conflict society. (7)

Theories put forward by Galtung (1976), Lederach (2005) and others have influenced some of the definitions of peacebuilding education adopted by international organisations, although UNICEF (2011) points out that peacebuilding theories did not have a strong enough influence on relevant educational programmes and that a thorough analysis of the role of education in peacebuilding is underdeveloped.

Indeed, there have been numerous efforts to review the divergent literature relating to the role of education in peacebuilding in order to develop a theoretically informed approach in the international realm (e.g. Save the Children 2008; UNESCO 2011; UNICEF 2011). The UNICEF (2011) review identified three distinctive areas of discourse when discussing the role of education in peacebuilding, whereby only the latter maps clearly onto the conceptualisation of peacebuilding as a process that may transform societies in the long-term: (1) education in emergencies, which concerns the protection of children and a response to the negative impacts of conflict on their education; (2) conflict-sensitive education that does not reinforce inequalities or fuel further divisions amongst people and communities; and (3) education that actively supports peacebuilding through reforms that contribute to political, economic and social transformations in post-conflict society and through a focus on change in attitude, values and norms. Similarly, Smith (2010) identifies distinctive roles of education within the overall context of peacebuilding: preventative, protective and transformative. The transformative role is particularly relevant to post-conflict societies, where education also has an explicit focus on cultivating students' sense of justice and peace and thereby changing individual attitudes as well as transforming society. The UNESCO International Commission on Education for the Twenty-First Century (Delors et al. 1996) proposes four main pillars of learning, including: 'learning to know', 'learning to do', 'learning to be' and 'learning to live together', thus emphasising a holistic concept of education and stressing the importance of education in building a more peaceful world.

Education has been proposed as a key component in societal healing (Smith and Vaux 2003), which ought to be given priority over macroeconomic and institutional reform in peacebuilding (Collier and Hoeffler 2002). Smith and Vaux (2003) add that education can provide a framework for teaching and learning about reconciliation that will have a long-term impact as it may help to avoid trans-generational transmission of societal trauma. Korostelina (2012) and McInnis (2008) explain that the transformative power of peacebuilding education lies in its potential to redress processes of dehumanisation, which are seen as root causes of societal violence and which also result in the denial of a group of people's moral values and human rights. Most of the reviews mentioned above also stress the potentially significant contribution of peacebuilding education in overcoming conflicted collective histories and past trauma; in the development and maintenance of a culture of tolerance, diversity and inclusion; and in the establishment and promotion of democratic citizenship and critical engagement with politics and society.

Whilst education is often described as an inherently positive force, attention has been drawn to the controversial 'two faces of education', whereby education may play both a positive and a negative role in conflict and in peacebuilding thereafter (Bush and Saltarelli 2000). Concerns have been raised about the destructive role of education in perpetuating the root causes of conflict, such as inequality, negative intergroup attitudes and exclusion. This is particularly relevant in contexts where community divisions are sustained through structural mechanisms, such as unequal access to education, uneven distribution of resources or segregation, as well as pedagogical ones, including the use of history and textbooks for cultural and political purposes, oppression and repression (Buckland 2004; Bush and Saltarelli 2000).

Peace-oriented educational aims, such as cultivating students' critical capacity to challenge inequality and injustice and developing their understanding of democracy and human rights, are considered to be in tension with formal education and schooling, which is seen as inextricably linked to the state and prevalent hegemonic powers (Bekerman 2012). Harber and Skade (2009) regard schools as, 'dehumanising institutions that stress cognitive forms of knowledge over the affective, and that play down important inter-personal skills' (184). Thus they question whether peacebuilding education can ever be, 'truly compatible with, or comfortably coexist with, formal education as currently constructed in many parts of the world' (184). Other reviews (Salmi 2000; Seitz 2004) have criticised formal education for its use of different forms of violence, including direct violence (e.g. corporal punishment, sexual abuse in schools), indirect violence (e.g. illiteracy, educational inequality), repressive violence (e.g. deprivation of political rights) and alienating violence (e.g. through curriculum content, exclusion of mother tongue and suppression of subject teaching). Vriens (2003) points out sharply that we must be suspicious about claims of education being the instrument for peace.

Adding to such concerns relating to formal educational settings is a perception of an over-emphasis of academic and public debates around peacebuilding education for children and young people, whereby the responsibility for societal transformation is not shouldered by adults, but by the future generation. Salomon and Cairns (2010) point out that, 'the decision to focus on children ignores the fact that power is in the hands of adults, and it is how this power is used that will determinate the type of society children will inherit' (2).

The conflicting roles of education in post-conflict and divided societies hence pose questions as to how education for peacebuilding can become a genuinely transformative process. Smith and Vaux (2003) argue that educational policies and practices must be critically examined in terms of their potential to aggravate or ameliorate conflict. Smith (2010) thus recommends that educational policies and programmes be actively adjusted to the needs of human development and include a re-thinking of educational governance, structures, content and pedagogies. Likewise, UNICEF (2011) proposes that critical questions must be posed to interrogate 'the form and content for education' and 'its implications for relations between peoples, groups and nations' (20) in order to ensure that it becomes an avenue for peace rather than conflict.

This brief survey of the divergent literature about the role of education in peacebuilding has brought to light the complexity of the field and the controversy in conceptualising the role of education in peacebuilding. Indeed, such intricacy and ambiguity is similarly reflected in pedagogical approaches to peacebuilding education, which are also infused by additional challenges due to varied initiatives that attract parallel educational discourses, as will be explored below.

Pedagogical approaches to peacebuilding education

In recent years, pedagogical strategies oriented towards peacebuilding have increasingly come to the forefront of educational policy and attracted attention from educational theorists and empirical researchers (Bickmore 2011). Despite this attention, pedagogical practices often remain unconnected from theoretical frameworks and only limited research has been conducted to examine the effectiveness of educational initiatives aimed at creating a culture of peace in schools and to transform wider society. Our focus here is to explore pedagogical features and practices across divergent peacebuilding education initiatives in order to analyse their conceptual underpinnings in the last part of the article.

There are some shared views amongst researchers in terms of what characterises peace-oriented pedagogy. Jenkins (2008) summarises that pedagogical strategies for peacebuilding must be aimed at, 'deep change affecting ways of thinking, worldviews, values, behaviours, relationships, and social structures' (167). Equally, Ardizzone (2002) argues for pedagogical practices that cultivate peace-oriented values and attitudes, which require 'a paradigm shift' (16) that shapes content and pedagogy and incorporates fundamental human concerns in the process of pedagogical development, such as security, justice, relationships, values and responsibilities. Dupuy (2008) adds that peace-oriented pedagogy ought to be characterised by cooperative learning environments, critical thinking, participation and dialogue. In contrast to education *about* peace as a knowledge-based approach, pedagogical approaches to peacebuilding therefore centre on education *for* peace, which is characterised by the development of capacities and cultivation of values, such as (re)humanisation, considered necessary for societal transformation and social harmony (Kester 2010; Reardon 1988).

Despite such commonalities in focus as highlighted by the literature relating to peacebuilding, the pedagogical field comprises a multitude of divergent initiatives in schools and communities and is far from unified (Andersson, Hinge, and Messina 2011). These divergent initiatives, in turn, are reflected in parallel and frequently unconnected academic policy and practitioner discourses relating to the role of education in promoting citizenship and democracy, human rights and shared values, or societal healing and reconciliation, and where peacebuilding is situated within these broad aims.

In light of such complexity, we will briefly review pedagogical practices embedded within those educational initiatives that have received attention in such discourses and that have been proposed as particularly relevant for societal transformation, namely citizenship education (Quaynor 2012; Smith 2003), values education (UNESCO 1998a), critical education (Reardon 2011) and history education (McCully 2012). We will focus our review in particular on the identification of key issues in implementing such pedagogical strategies for peacebuilding.

Citizenship education

Despite criticisms that civic and citizenship education could be used as a means of nation-building and assimilation (Smith 2010), many of its modern proponents conceptualise it as an approach to cultivating shared values, democratic skills and inclusive attitudes and to framing citizenship and identity in terms of human rights, respect for diversity and civic responsibilities (Davies 2004; Hughes et al. 2010; Niens and Reilly 2012; Torney-Purta et al. 2001; USAID 2002). As such, countries around the world have incorporated citizenship education in different ways into formal educational curricula (Schulz et al. 2010).

While the actual implementation of citizenship education varies substantially across and within nations, it is often understood by teachers as primarily relating to acquiring knowledge (e.g. about political institutions) and skills (e.g. communication skills) rather than fostering values, participation and engagement (Schulz et al. 2010). An important aspect of citizenship education, however, is active citizenship modelled and lived by the staff and students in the implicit and informal curriculum, social relationships, classroom climate and the practices of equity, fairness and justice in an overall school structure (Bickmore 2005). While this aspect of citizenship education is recognised to some extent, the lesser emphasis placed on it in comparison to knowledge may be explained by suggestions that active engagement and inquiry-based pedagogy for citizenship education, 'runs counter to the prevailing curriculum, which is predominantly content-based and dominated by subject disciplines' (Smith 2003, 26).

As such, it may not be surprising that research has identified that political participation in schools as a pedagogical strategy of active citizenship is not always possible (Akar 2006; Dean 2005; Faour and Muasher 2011;

Kester 2010). This is because such political participation challenges existing power relations, structures and institutional cultures within a school system that maintains a purpose of education as reproduction rather than transformation of society (Bourdieu and Passeron 1990; Collins 2009). At the same time, whilst empowering approaches to citizenship education require teachers/educators to model a democratic climate within the learning environment (Bickmore 2005; UNESCO 1998a), they pose further challenges to teachers whose training may have been narrowly focused on teaching a prescriptive curriculum or whose teaching may contradict their own beliefs or those of the community around them (Quaynor 2012). This may be amplified in the context of societies overcoming political conflict. Shuayb (2007) illustrates through her research in Lebanese schools that during civic lessons, students are imparted information and knowledge about democratic practice and critical dialogue, and yet in their day-to-day reality, there is no 'chance to experience and live within a democratic environment in school' (182). Her finding is echoed by Akar (2006), who asserts that:

> [t]he inconsistencies between home, school and society and the need for dialogue in a contents-based civics curriculum continue to challenge effective citizenship education in Lebanon ... (61)

Quaynor's (2012) literature review on citizenship education in post-conflict countries identifies a common tendency amongst teachers to avoid critical reflection and discourse about political issues and inequalities in such contexts. It also highlights a central role for reflection on ethnic and national identities in citizenship education in order for it to be meaningful in post-conflict and divided societies. Whilst an emphasis on identities has long been embedded in peacebuilding education, Bekerman and Zembylas (2011) warn that this may in fact serve to essentialise identities and reinforce perceptions of intergroup boundaries. Thus, Smith (2003) proposes that engaging in critical discourse about past, present and future identities and their socially constructed nature ought to be one element of citizenship education, where students with divergent perspectives embark on a process of imagining future positive peace beyond identity divisions. This constructivist approach to identities, social categories and their cultural meanings may thus provide the first step in a pedagogical dialogue that may disrupt 'us and them' perceptions of collectives and thereby (re)humanise 'the other'.

Values education

Rooted in moral and religious education, values education is sometimes seen as part of citizenship education, but is increasingly becoming a curriculum and pedagogical focus in its own right (Funk 2012; UNESCO 1998b). Its pedagogical practices tend to centre on promoting values and concepts of virtues that are believed to be accepted across cultures and societies (Farrer 2000). It is based on the conviction that values are necessary to improve the quality of an individual's life and that of the whole society and that they thus represent a foundation for peace (Carr 1997).

Given the aforementioned constraints of frequently reproductive education systems and authoritarian school structures, values education has been criticised for imposing majority viewpoints where it should be value-neutral to protect plurality of values (Lovat and Toomey 2009). Indeed, some research indicates that dialogic approaches to values education integrated in student-centred, participatory and peer-mediated pedagogies may fit more easily into some indigenous education formats, where educational structures may be less rigid, and post-conflict societies, where traditional values may have been eroded (e.g. Rwantabagu 2010).

Similar to citizenship education, values education confronts teachers with a key challenge: teachers not only need to have an explicit understanding of the values they promote, but they must also integrate such values in their own life and work. In other words, teachers/educators must practise what they preach. Thus, teachers' personal and professional growth is considered to be part of the pedagogical approach. Coles (1997) suggests that, '[w]e grow morally as a consequence of learning how to be with others, how to behave in this world, a learning prompted by taking to heart what we have seen and heard' (5).

Values education is confronted with particular challenges in the context of societies experiencing violent conflict, such as Palestine, and Affouneh (2007) argues that children cannot learn and act on human values when they are 'exposed to violence and hatred and the associated feelings of fear, anger and hopelessness' (354). In turn, it may be suggested that teachers, equally, find it difficult to act as role models in such contexts.

UNESCO (2002) explores values education in the context of 'Learning to be', where the educative process is 'both holistic and integrative' and where 'valuing' starts from the micro-environment (home, classroom) to the macro-environment (society, nation, globe and cosmic). It is argued that, 'only in this very context will the learner truly experience the art of being fully human, instead of learning it merely as an idea and/or ideal' (12). UNESCO (1998b) claims that values education can counteract some of the criticisms levelled at many educational initiatives aimed at peacebuilding, which are often regarded as imposing Western values (Gur Ze'ev 2001) and that values education actually balances 'Eastern' and 'Western', 'traditional' and 'modern', 'secular' and 'religious' perspectives. However, the question remains as to how this balance can be maintained. Acknowledging the often controversial nature of values where they are in tension with each other, UNESCO (1998b, 172) considers values education as 'philosophy in practice' and recommends that values education be introduced through diverse pedagogical strategies, including the clarification of values, posing and resolving moral dilemmas through discourse, critical analysis, action learning and, above all, modelling and living values. Embedded in such pedagogical strategies is the consistent need for 'hermeneutical approaches' that promote dialogue and encounter with others within diverse contexts (Jackson and Fujiwara 2007) and thus engender humanisation.

Critical education

Critical education has been regarded as having roots in critical theory (such as the Frankfurt School of Sociology), Freire's pedagogy of the oppressed and Dewey's theory of democratic education (Jenkins 2008). Arguing against broad and often diffuse definitions of critical education in the literature, Apple, Au, and Gandin (2009) highlight that the challenge to unequal power relationships is at its core and that critical education needs to incorporate re-thinking what, how and why we teach and learn. As such, critical education has been integrated in peacebuilding education (Bickmore 1993; Reardon 2011; Reardon and Snauwaert 2011) because it poses an explicit criticism of the social structures and power dynamics with the goal to address violence (Giroux 1997; Harris 2004). Some writers have started to refer to 'critical peace education' where it aims to cultivate critical consciousness that serves to address the need to understand the roots of violence and, at the same time, create optimism and hope (Bajaj 2008).

Reflection and dialogue are core components of critical education for peacebuilding. According to Andersson, Hinge, and Messina (2011), a dialogic approach to critical education involves listening, posing genuine questions and collaborative inquiry, which serve as the basis for developing critical thinking and for shifting one's own views and understanding. Bajaj (2008) suggests that when students engage in critical dialogue and reflection, they may overcome intergroup divisions and ultimately transform relationships between people from communities in conflict.

The critical pedagogical framework is proposed as a broadly transformative agenda where, 'moral and political agency come together to inspire both a discourse of hope and a political project that takes seriously what it means to envision a better life and society' (Giroux 1988, 38). Within such a framework, the pedagogical intention is to enable students to think critically and act collectively in order to build a more peaceful society. This includes becoming aware of the institutional obstacles (in schools and in society at large) that may hinder societal transformation beyond inequalities and conflict boundaries. Critical education is thus clearly transformative in its theoretical underpinnings and influenced by Freirean notions of dialogue and humanisation. It could be seen as bringing together modern notions of citizenship education, with its transformative political agenda, and values education, with its focus on beliefs, values, personal growth and social relationships.

Despite these strengths in addressing a broad agenda for peacebuilding, critical education also suffers from some of the criticisms levelled at both citizenship and values education, in that it implicitly assumes a shared and universal values base, whereby tensions and differences in values may be overlooked, and goodwill in the political, societal and educational arenas, which in reality may often be curtailed by vested interests in divisions and conflict (Giroux 1988).

History education

Many scholars have advocated that history education can provide an important pedagogical tool for developing social cohesion (Larkin 2012). Collective memories and narratives have been regarded as key concepts for re-consolidating identities and thereby meaning and purpose of communities (Goodson and Gill 2010; Hammack and Pilecki 2012). In post-conflict societies, history education may address the need to deal with past violence and divergent notions of history and provide students with the opportunity to explore how their own identities and communities are located in a larger (national and international) history (Cole and Barsalou 2006). In such contexts, where issues relating to identity and past trauma are particularly prominent, collective narratives and memories appear to play contrasting roles: on the one hand, they can be used to justify violence and injustice, perpetuate cycles of violence and reinforce identities that divide society (Bar-Tal 2003; Moses 1991), resulting in demonising collective narratives and memories at the roots of conflict and violence (Wang 2009). As such, there has been increased recognition that unresolved disagreements about historical narratives can lead to renewed conflict and/or violence (Korostelina and Lässig 2013). On the other hand, they can form the basis for creating hope and envisioning a shared destiny amongst different communities in peace and solidarity (Lederach 2005), highlighting the narrative's humanising potential. Sharing of collective narratives and memories across community boundaries has thus been proposed as a pedagogical approach to history education in post-conflict societies in order to break the cycles of violence by transforming anger and resentment into the ability to empathise with the perspective of the other and to develop the opportunity of living together in dignity and peace (Borer 2006).

Research into history education in Northern Ireland suggests that a shared history curriculum may be valuable in presenting alternative perspectives and challenging students' attitudes towards the 'other' (McCully 2012). This is echoed by educators in Asia who explored collective history writing with young people from China, Japan and the Republic of Korea to collaborate and produce a history textbook that honours collective memories of all sides (Wang 2009).

Despite the suggested benefits of history education, pedagogies aimed at addressing divergent narratives, identities and traumas remain difficult to implement within educational institutions due to the controversial nature of such approaches in conflicted societies (Salomon and Haggai 2005). Additionally, teachers are often challenged to present alternative perspectives, which may be contrary to their own and those of the communities around them, whereby they may lack empathy themselves with these divergent views (Barton and McCully 2012).

The paradoxical feature of collective narratives poses a challenge to history education for peacebuilding (McKnight 2004). Where history education appears to play a constructive role in conflict, pedagogical approaches tend to be characterised by the analysis of divergent narratives and interpretations that frame memories of the past within specific historical conditions rather than objective and static truth (Papadakis 2008). Such approaches stress the socially constructed nature of identities and communities as well as the suffering of others. Classroom implementation of these approaches to history education tends to be dialogic, including perspective taking, listening and critical thinking, which resemble those applied in citizenship education (Shuayb 2012), as well as open enquiries, critical analysis of memorials, museums or truth commissions (Cole and Barsalou 2006). The process of 'creative re-storying' of collective memories has been suggested to be transformative in nature by not merely promoting a shared understanding of the past (Cole and Barsalou 2006), but also a vision of present and future peace, including questioning who we are, where we belong, where we are going and how we can journey together (Lederach 2005).

In summary

Based on our review of pedagogical approaches to peacebuilding education, we propose two tentative conclusions: (1) dialogic pedagogical practices for the broad aim of peacebuilding through humanisation are characterised by fostering respect for human dignity, reconciliation and relation-building, celebrating shared humanity as our common identity and reconstructing a vision for a humane society where there is the possibility of a culture of peace; and (2) in many post-conflict societies, the existing educational systems, including the overall educational vision, institutional structure within schools, classroom climate and teacher education, need to shift in order to accommodate dialogic pedagogy as a key element for peacebuilding education and to transform society.

Whilst implementing a humanising approach and critical dialogue in peacebuilding education appears to require further conceptual debate and empirical investigation, there seems to be scope to take a closer look at the philosophical underpinning of dialogic pedagogy that emerged as a theoretical framework unifying the peacebuilding pedagogies in the divergent educational initiatives reviewed above.

Dialogic humanising pedagogy in education for peacebuilding – reaffirming a theoretical framework

While Galtung (1975) claimed that there was no comprehensive and practical theory for peace-oriented education, three decades later our review of the pedagogical approaches to peacebuilding education suggests a converging conceptualisation of peacebuilding education as dialogic, humanising and transformative. Indeed, the peacebuilding theories and pedagogies surveyed above all incorporate an element of critical reflection and dialogue, inquiry-based learning and authentic relationships in the process of education and hermeneutical encounter, which are regarded as the foundation of participatory, emancipatory and transformative education (Freire 1996, 2004).

Education as humanisation

Peacebuilding education requires a pedagogical focus on dealing with the past (and healing the wounds of violent and traumatic events), repairing and rebuilding human relationships and raising an awareness of human values (Salomon 2011). Whilst rarely explicitly applied to theoretical conceptualisations of peacebuilding education, and even less so to pedagogical practice, Freire's ideas have been proposed as addressing these concerns and as the most illuminating in transformative peace-oriented education (Reardon 2009).

Freire (1996) maintains that education 'consists in permitting the emergence of the awareness of our full humanity' (74–75). The 'Pedagogy of the Oppressed' aims to enable those who are oppressed to critically discover that they and their oppressors are manifestations of dehumanisation. Therefore, the ultimate end of liberation is seen as the humanisation of all people, both the oppressed and the oppressors, which is not 'a mere reversal of position … [or] the replacement of the former oppressors with new ones who continue to subjugate the oppressed' (39). In this way, individuals and communities are believed to be able to engage in the 'ontological and historical vocation of becoming more fully human' (48).

For Freire (1996), education must be a collaborative process of reciprocal relationships between the educator and educatee. Critical consciousness is the critical reflection on one's own, 'existential experience and human-world relationship and on the relationship between people implicit in the former' (78). He further argues that the key to emancipation and conflict transformation involves a three-pronged integral process of humanisation, including critical reflection, dialogue and action. Thus, critical reflection, which is developed through dialogue, is proposed to enable us to identify, and ultimately challenge, the contexts and circumstances that may prevent us from becoming human.

Humanisation has long been integral to philosophical considerations relating to the aims of education (e.g. Dewey 1939; Gill and Thomson 2012). Bartolome (1994) proposed the term 'humanising pedagogy', which has recently been expanded by Keet, Zinn, and Porteus (2009) to especially address education in post-conflict peacebuilding. Shapiro (2002) joins Freire in proposing a pedagogy of love and compassion, highlighting that humanising education may help to develop just and equal societies as it 'speaks, after all, to that profound quality that connects and unites human beings while, or after, all our distinctions have been given their due recognition' (69–70).

Education as humanisation has thus influenced the values underpinning peacebuilding education and we argue here that it may offer a framework to unite the different pedagogical elements reviewed above.

Dialogue as humanising pedagogy

Freire (1996) defines dialogue as: 'the encounter between men, mediated by the world, in order to name the world' (69). Language is hence seen as central in dialogue, and for it to have critical quality, and thereby to be transformative, it must be authentic, reflective, problem-posing and committed to action for change. For Freire, denying people's rights and opportunity to express themselves through language and to act so as to change the world is dehumanising because he sees dialogue (and reflection and action) as a necessity for all human beings. This is similar to Dewey (1916), who views dialogic encounters as satisfying a common human need in overcoming isolation and engendering emotional closeness. Such encounters are assumed to allow us to form intense friendships, and it is through such encounters that a community is believed to take shape. It therefore provides an important component in the development of a peaceful and democratic culture – a process of being and living together in and through dialogic and communicated experience (Dewey 1939).

Freire's understanding of dialogue centres on notions of love, hope, humility and critical analysis, which are proposed to enable positive transformation of the self, interpersonal relationships and society. Freire (1996) sees the motivation for transforming the world for the liberation of humankind as based on a belief in humanity and a 'profound love for the world and for people' (70). Love and hope are considered the basis for taking the courage to act in order to create a new vision of the world, which challenges power imbalances and breaks down social barriers of class, gender and ethnicity. In his view, as individuals transform the world, they transform themselves within it (Freire 1996). Thus, at the heart of Freire's thesis lies the primacy of a universal human ethic, a vision of the good and a quest for unfolding human potential, which he believed underpins all human relationships and actions (Freire 2004).

Acknowledging the significance of human relationships, Buber (1923/2008) already highlighted the role of critical dialogue for 'I and thou' relationships and for conflict resolution between communities (Morgan and Guilherme 2012, 2). Whilst Buber (1965/1988) suggests that the notion of 'we' can only develop in the human encounter through critical dialogue, Bakhtin cautions that this is only one possible outcome and that dialogue may run in parallel tracks, never coming to a mutual agreement (Thompson 2012). In order for dialogue to become meaningful, it must involve and engender critical consciousness, which uncovers and questions implicit assumptions and challenges the status quo (Sammel 2003). What is crucial here is the suggestion that dialogue requires the critical and, at the same time, engenders the critical. In the context of peacebuilding education, dialogic pedagogy is thus hoped to raise students' consciousness about divergent narratives and oppressive social structures, criticise power imbalances, develop shared understandings of the past, present and future and expand the classroom practices in order to cultivate teachers' and students' capacity to act as agents of change (Kincheloe 2004; McLaren 2000). In this way, critical humanising pedagogy aims to unmask the world and then change it and individual emancipation is seen as contingent to social transformation (Giroux 1988, 1997).

Dialogic humanising pedagogy has thus been proposed as an avenue for change through relationship building and through tackling those social political issues that are at the roots of violence. It is situated within a holistic vision of peace as a sustainable but transformative process and promises a continued humanising and emancipatory journey of peacebuilding. While critical dialogic methods in education have been heralded as an important way forward to bridging diversity and promoting equality, Burbules (2000, 8) cautioned that '[t]he very aim of dialogue to speak and understand across differences is not an unalloyed benefit to all potential parties to such dialogue' and that it actually may be a vehicle for assimilation of difference into mainstream beliefs. Given that criticality is always social in nature (Burbules and Berk 1999), such fears of assimilation and erosion of difference may be particularly relevant in the context of post-conflict societies, where cultural differences and divergent narratives may represent different communities' understandings of the past as well as the present and future. As such, the potential of critical dialogue in education in such contexts may not only be curtailed by Freire's notion of 'banking education', but even more so by the wider societal context of community divisions, which may pervade communities, politics and the media so that, in reality, educational efforts may only provide small opportunities to briefly interrupt the common discourse of difference. Indeed, Salomon (2011) suggests that two of the most important challenges for peacebuilding education in post-conflict societies remain the extent to which such initiatives may transform deeply held beliefs and values (rather than peripheral attitudes) and the extent to which any impact may last over time.

Conclusion: pedagogy for peacebuilding education

In this article, we provided an overview of relevant literature in the field of peacebuilding education, which revealed conceptual gaps and a lack of integrated theories. A further exploration of existing pedagogical practices and strategies in the field suggested that these are often underscored by a convergence of conceptual arguments that implicitly incorporate a humanising and transformative agenda as proposed by Freire and others. We argue that the lack of explicit recognition of dialogic and humanising pedagogical influences has resulted in theoretical ambiguity relating to key concepts. This no doubt precludes the field of peacebuilding education developing and implementing more rigorous empirical research that could bridge the frequently cited gap between theory, research and educational practice. Only by moving the field forward through such empirical research will we be able to highlight effective teaching pedagogies for peacebuilding in a variety of different socio-political and educational contexts. While education for peacebuilding has often been criticised for its Western roots and accused of a neo-colonial agenda that imposes Western notions of peacebuilding (Wessels 2013), explicitly acknowledging the voices and influences of those from the Global South, such as Paulo Freire, may help to address some of the inequalities in academic discourses relating to education for sustainable peace and to take account of widely divergent socio-political and cultural contexts. The central role of critical discourses within peacebuilding education should thus not only be seen as a matter for teaching in the classroom, but for a humanising discourse between educationalists and academics that goes beyond neo-colonial and top-down approaches and acknowledges local and contextual values and knowledge (Wessels 2013).

In order to consolidate the significance and impact of humanising and dialogic pedagogies in peacebuilding education, we conclude that it is thus crucial to subject the practices and theories to critical and systematic research, to improve educational practice and to develop effective peacebuilding education strategies. In particular, the Janus face of education with regard to its potential to catalyse division or promote peace must be acknowledged when questioning whether education should and can represent the main societal vehicle for change in the context of conflict and division.

However, we would argue that education is a key place to start in promoting a humanising and transformative agenda but only as part of wider social, political and economic strategies for peacebuilding and reconstruction. Otherwise, education aimed at challenging inequalities, addressing root causes of violence and promoting societal transformation will fall short in achieving its potential where societal and educational structures, policies and discourses continue to reiterate divisions and conflict. Whilst any attempt of peacebuilding education may be fraught with difficulties and subject to wider debate, it also creates an opportunity for more rigorous investigation and analysis.

References

Affouneh, S. 2007. "How Sustained Conflict Makes Moral Education Impossible: Some Observations from Palestine." *Journal of Moral Education* 36 (3): 343–356.

Akar, B. 2006. "Teachers' Reflections on the Challenges of Teaching Citizenship Education in Lebanon: A Qualitative Pilot Study." *Reflecting Education* 2 (2): 48–63.

Andersson, I., H. Hinge, and C. Messina. 2011. *Peace Education: Children's Identity & Citizenship in Europe Guidebook*. London: Erasmus Academic Network.

Apple, M. W., W. Au, and L. A. Gandin. 2009. "Mapping Critical Education." *The Routledge International Handbook of Critical Education*, edited by M. W. Apple, W. Au, and L. A. Gandin, 3–20. Abingdon/New York: Routledge.

Ardizzone, L. 2002. "Towards Global Understanding: The Transformative Role of Peace Education." *Current Issues in Comparative Education* 4 (2): 16–25.

Bajaj, M. 2004. "Human Rights Education and Student Self-Conception in the Dominican Republic." *Journal of Peace Education* 1 (1): 21–36.

Bajaj, M. 2008. "'Critical' Peace Education." In *Encyclopaedia of Peace Education*, edited by M. Bajaj, 135–144. Charlotte, NC: Information Age.

Bar-Tal, D. 2003. "Collective Memory of Physical Violence: Its Contribution to the Culture of Violence." In *The Role of Memory in Ethnic Conflict*, edited by E. Cairns and M. Roe, 77–93. New York: Palgrave Macmillan.

Bartolome, L. 1994. "Beyond the Methods Fetish: Toward a Humanizing Pedagogy." *Harvard Educational Review* 64 (2): 173–194.

Barton, K. C., and A. W. McCully. 2012. "Trying to 'See Things Differently': Northern Ireland Students' Struggle to Understand Alternative Historical Perspectives." *Theory & Research in Social Education* 40 (4): 371–408.

Bekerman, Z. 2012. "Afterword: Reflecting on Critical Perspectives of Peace Education." In *Educating for Peace in a Time of War: Are Schools Part of the Solution or the Problem?* edited by P. R. Carr and B. J. Porfilio, 271–278. Abingdon, UK: Routledge.

Bekerman, Z., and M. Zembylas. 2011. *Teaching Contested Narratives*. Cambridge: Cambridge University Press.

Bickmore, K. 1993. "Learning Inclusion/Inclusion in Learning: Citizenship Education for a Pluralistic Society." *Theory and Research in Social Education* 21 (4): 341–384.

Bickmore, K. 2005. "Teacher Development for Conflict Participation: Facilitating Learning for 'Difficult Citizenship' Education." *International Journal of Citizenship and Teacher Education* 1 (2): 2–14.

Bickmore, K. 2011. "Peacebuilding Dialogue as Democratic Education: Conflictual Issues, Restorative Problem-Solving, and Student Diversity in Classrooms." In

Debates in Citizenship Education, edited by J. Arthur and H. Cremin, 115–131. New York, NY: Routledge.

Borer, T. ed. 2006. *Telling the Truth: Truth Telling and Peace-Building in Post-Conflict Societies*. Notre Dame, IN: University of Notre Dame Press.

Bourdieu, P., and J. C. Passeron. 1990. *Reproduction in Education, Society and Culture*. London: Sage.

Buber, M. 1923/2008. *Ich Und Du. Mit Einem Nachwort Von Bernhard Casper*. Stuttgart: Reclam.

Buber, M. 1965/1988. *The Knowledge of Man: A Philosophy of the Interhuman*. Translated by Maurice Friedman and Ronald Gregor Smith. Edited by Maurice Friedman. Amherst and New York: Prometheus Books.

Buckland, P. 2004. *Reshaping the Future: Education and Post-Conflict Reconstruction*. Washington, DC: World Bank.

Burbules, N. C. 2000. "The Limits of Dialogue as a Critical Pedagogy." In *Revolutionary Pedagogies: Cultural Politics, Instituting Education, and the Discourse of Theory*, edited by P. Trifonas, 251–273. New York: Routledge.

Burbules, N. C., and R. Berk. 1999. "Critical Thinking and Critical Pedagogy: Relations, Differences, and Limits." In *Critical Theories in Education*, edited by T. S. Popkewitz and L. Fendler, 45–66. New York: Routledge.

Bush, K., and D. Saltarelli. 2000. *The Two Faces of Education in Ethnic Conflict: Towards a Peacebuilding Education for Children*. Florence, Italy: UNICEF.

Carr, D. 1997. "Educational Values and Values Education: Some Recent Work." *British Journal of Sociology of Education* 18 (1): 133–141.

Cole, E., and J. Barsalou. 2006. *Unite or Divide? The Challenges of Teaching History in Societies Emerging from Violent Conflict, Special Report 163*. Washington, DC: United States Institute of Peace.

Coles, R. 1997. *The Moral Development of Children*. New York: Random House.

Collier, C., and A. Hoeffler. 2002. "Aid, Policy and Growth in Post-Conflict Societies." World Bank Policy Research Working Paper 2902. Washington, DC: World Bank.

Collins, J. 2009. "Social Reproduction in Classrooms and Schools." *Annual Review of Anthropology* 38: 33–48.

Davies, L. 2004. *Education and Conflict: Complexity and Chaos*. New York: Routledge.

Dean, B. 2005. "Citizenship Education in Pakistani Schools: Problems and Possibilities." *International Journal of Citizenship and Teacher Education* 1 (2): 35–55.

Delors, J., I. Al Mufti, I. Amagi, R. Carneiro, F. Chung, B. Geremek, W. Gorham, et al. 1996. *Learning: The Treasure Within: Report to UNESCO of the International Commission on Education for the 21st Century*. Paris, France: UNESCO.

Dewey, J. 1916. *Democracy and Education. An Introduction to the Philosophy of Education*. New York: Free Press.

Dewey, J. 1939. *Freedom and Culture*. New York: Putnam.

Dupuy, K. 2008. *Education for Peace*. Oslo: International Peace Research Institute (PRIO) and Save the Children Norway.

Faour, M., and M. Muasher. 2011. *Education for Citizenship in the Arab World: Key to the Future*. The Carnegie Papers. Washington, DC: Carnegie Middle East Centre, Carnegie Endowment for International Peace.

Farrer, F. 2000. *A Quiet Revolution: Encouraging Positive Values in Our Children*. London: Rider.

Freire, P. 1996. *Pedagogy of the Oppressed*. London: Penguin Books.

Freire, P. 2004. *Pedagogy of Hope: Reliving Pedagogy of the Oppressed*. London: Continuum.
Funk, N. 2012. "Building on What's Already There: Valuing the Local in International Peacebuilding." *International Journal: Canada's Journal of Global Policy Analysis* 67 (2): 391–408.
Galtung, J. 1975. *Peace: Research, Education, Action. Essays in Peace Research*. Vol. I. Copenhagen: Christan Ejlers.
Galtung, J. 1976. "Three Approaches to Peace: Peacekeeping, Peacemaking, Peacebuilding." In *Peace, War and Defense: Essays in Peace Research*, Vol. II, edited by J. Galtung, 297–298. Copenhagen: Christian Ejlers.
Gill, S., and G. Thomson. 2012. *Rethinking Secondary Education: A Human-Centred Approach*. London: Pearson Education.
Giroux, H. 1988. *Schooling for Democracy: Critical Pedagogy in the Modern Age*. London: Routledge.
Giroux, H. 1997. *Pedagogy and the Politics of Hope*. Boulder, CO: Westview Press.
Goodson, I., and S. Gill. 2010. *Narrative Pedagogy*. New York: Peter Lang.
Gur Ze'ev, I. 2001. "Philosophy of Peace Education in a Postmodern Era." *Educational Theory* 51 (3): 315–336.
Hammack, P. L., and A. Pilecki. 2012. "Narrative as a Root Metaphor for Political Psychology." *Political Psychology* 33 (1): 75–103.
Hansen, D. T., S. Burdick-Shepherd, C. Cammarano, and G. Obelleiro. 2009. "Education, Values, and Valuing in Cosmopolitan Perspective." *Curriculum Inquiry* 39 (5): 587–612.
Harber, C., and N. Skade. 2009. "Schooling for Violence and Peace: How Does Peace Education Differ from 'Normal' Schooling?" *Journal of Peace Education* 6 (2): 171–187.
Harris, I. 2004. "Peace Education Theory." *Journal of Peace Education* 1 (1): 5–20.
Hughes, A., M. Print, and A. Sears. 2010. "Curriculum Capacity and Citizenship Education: A Comparative Analysis of Four Democracies." *Compare* 40 (3): 293–309.
Jackson, R., and S. Fujiwara. 2007. "Towards Religious Education for Peace." *British Journal of Religious Education.* 29 (1): 1–14.
Jenkins, T. 2008. "The International Institute on Peace Education: Twenty-Six Years Modelling Critical, Participatory Peace Pedagogy." *Journal of Peace Education and Social Justice* 2 (2): 166–174.
Keet, A., D. Zinn, and K. Porteus. 2009. "Mutual Vulnerability: A Key Principle in a Humanising Pedagogy in Post-Conflict Societies." *Perspectives in Education* 27 (2): 109–119.
Kester, K. 2010. "Education for Peace: Content, Form, and Structure: Mobilizing Youth for Civic Engagement." *Peace & Conflict Review* 4 (2): 1–10.
Kincheloe, J. 2004. *Critical Pedagogy*. New York: Peter Lang.
Korostelina, K. 2012. *Forming a Culture of Peace*. New York: Palgrave Macmillan.
Korostelina, K., and S. Lässig, eds. 2013. *History Education and Post-Conflict Reconciliation: Reconsidering Joint Textbook Projects*. London: Routledge.
Lambourne, W. 2004. "Post-Conflict Peacebuilding: Meeting Human Needs for Justice and Reconciliation." *Peace, Conflict and Development* 4: 1–24.
Larkin, C. 2012. *Memory and Conflict in Lebanon: Remembering and Forgetting the past*. Abingdon, Oxon: Routledge.

Lederach, J.-P. 1998. "Beyond Violence: Building Sustainable Peace." In *The Handbook of Interethnic Coexistence*, edited by E. Weiner, 236–245. New York: Continuum.

Lederach, J.-P. 2003. *The Little Book of Conflict Transformation*. Intercourse, PA: Good Books.

Lederach, J.-P. 2005. *The Moral Imagination*. Oxford: Oxford University Press.

Lovat, T., and R. Toomey. 2009. "Introduction: Values Education – a Brief History to Today." In *Values Education and Quality Teaching*, edited by T. Lovat and R. Toomey, xi–xviii. Dordrecht: Springer.

Maiese, M. 2003. "Peacebuilding." *Beyond Intractability*. Accessed May 2012. www.beyondintractability.org

McCully, A. 2012. "History Teaching, Conflict and the Legacy of the Past." *Education, Citizenship and Social Justice* 7 (2): 145–159.

McInnis, D. 2008. "A Nonviolent Response to Terrorism: What Can Peace Education Do?" In *Nonviolence: An Alternative for Defeating Global Terror (Ism)*, edited by S. Ram and R. Summy, 145–168. Hauppauge, NY: Nova Science.

McKnight, A. 2004. "Historical Trauma, the Persistence of Memory and the Pedagogical Problems of Forgiveness, Justice and Peace." *Educational Studies* 36 (2): 140–158.

McLaren, P. 2000. "Paulo Freire's Pedagogy of Possibility." In *Freirean Pedagogy, Praxis and Possibilities: Projects for the New Millennium*, edited by S. Steiner, H. M. Krank, P. McLaren, and R. E. Bahruth, 1–21. New York: Falmer Press.

Mitchell, G. 2003. "Inter-Cultural Education for Democracy: The Case of South Africa." In *Citizenship, Democracy and Lifelong Learning*, edited by C. Medel-Anonuevo and G. Mitchell, 153–167. Hamburg, Germany: UNESCO Institute for Education.

Morgan, W. J., and A. Guilherme. 2012. "*I and Thou*: The Educational Lessons of Martin Buber's Dialogue with the Conflicts of His Times." *Educational Philosophy and Theory* 44 (2): 979–996.

Morris, C. 2000. *What is Peacebuilding: One Definition*. Victoria, BC, Canada: Peacebuilding Trust. Accessed January 2013. http://www.peacemakers.ca/publications/peacebuildingdefinition.html

Moses, R. 1991. "On Dehumanizing the Enemy." In *The Psychodynamics of International Relations: Volume II*, edited by V. Volkan, J. Montville, and D. Julius, 117–125. Lexington, MA: D.C. Heath, Lexington Books.

Niens, U., and J. Reilly. 2012. "Education for Global Citizenship in a Divided Society? Young People's Views and Experiences." *Comparative Education* 48 (1): 103–118.

Oxfam. 2008. *From Emergency to Recovery: Rescuing Northern Uganda's Transition*. Oxford: Oxfam International.

Papadakis, Y. 2008. "Narrative, Memory and History Education in Divided Cyprus: A Comparison of Schoolbooks on the 'History of Cyprus'." *Journal of History & Memory* 20 (2): 128–148.

Quaynor, L. 2012. "Citizenship Education in Post-Conflict Contexts: A Review of the Literature." *Education, Citizenship and Social Justice* 7 (1): 33–57.

Reardon, B. 1988. *Comprehensive Peace Education: Educating for Global Responsibility*. New York: Teachers College Press.

Reardon, B. 2009. "Human Rights Learning: Pedagogies and Politics of Peace." Lecture delivered for the UNESCO Chair for Peace Education Masters Conference at the University of Puerto Rico, April 15.

Reardon, B. 2011. "Meditating on the Barricades: Concerns, Cautions and Possibilities for Peace Education for Political Efficacy." In *Critical Peace Education: Difficult Dialogue*, edited by B. Wright and P. Trifonas, 1–28. Boulder, CO: Springer.

Reardon, B., and D. Snauwaert. 2011. "Reflective Pedagogy, Cosmopolitanism, and Critical Peace Education for Political Efficacy: A Discussion of Betty A. Reardon's Assessment of the Field." *In Factis Pax* 5 (1): 1–14.

Rwantabagu, H. 2010. "Moral Education in a Post-Conflict Context: The Case of Burundi." *Journal of Moral Education* 39 (3): 345–352.

Salmi, J. 2000. *Violence, Democracy and Education: An Analytic Framework*. LCSHD Paper Series No. 56. Washington, DC: The World Bank.

Salomon, G. 2011. "Four Major Challenges Facing Peace Education in Regions of Intractable Conflict." *Peace and Conflict* 17 (1): 46–59.

Salomon, G., and E. Cairns. 2010. "Introduction." In *Handbook on Peace Education*, edited by G. Salomon and E. Cairns, 1–10. New York: Psychology Press.

Salomon, G., and K. Haggai. 2005. "Lessons to Be Learned from Research on Peace Education in the Context of Intractable Conflict." *Theory into Practice* 44 (4): 293–302.

Sammel, A. 2003. "An Invitation to Dialogue: Gadamer, Hermeneutic Phenomenology, and Critical Environmental Education." *Canadian Journal of Environmental Education* 8 (1): 155–168.

Save the Children. 2008. *Where Peace Begins: Education's Role in Conflict Prevention and Peacebuilding*. London: Save the Children.

Schulz, W., J. Ainley, J. Fraillon, D. Kerr, and B. Losito. 2010. *Initial Findings from the IEA International Civic and Citizenship Education Study*. Amsterdam: IEA.

Seitz, K. 2004. *Education and Conflict: The Role of Education in the Creation, Prevention and Resolution of Societal Crises – Consequences for Development Cooperation*. Rossdorff: German Technical Cooperation.

Shapiro, S. 2002. "Pedagogy of Peace Education." In *Peace Education: The Concept, Principles, and Practices around the World*, edited by G. Salomon and B. Nevo, 63–72. Mahwah, NJ: Lawrence Erlbaum Associates.

Shuayb, M. 2007. "Education – A Means for the Cohesion of the Lebanese Confessional Society." In *Breaking the Cycle*, edited by Y. Choueiri, 167–195. London: Stacey International.

Shuayb, M. ed. 2012. *Rethinking Education for Social Cohesion: International Case Studies*. Houndmills, Basingstoke: Palgrave Macmillan.

Smith, A. 2003. "Citizenship Education in Northern Ireland: Beyond National Identity?" *Cambridge Journal of Education* 33 (1): 15–31.

Smith, A. 2010. *The Influence of Education on Conflict and Peace Building, Background Paper Prepared for the Education for All Global Monitoring Report 2011*. Paris: UNESCO.

Smith, A., and T. Vaux. 2003. *Education, Conflict, and International Development*. London: Department of International Development.

Thompson, P. 2012. "Both Dialogic and Dialectic: 'Translation at the Crossroads'." *Learning, Culture and Social Interaction* 1 (2): 90–101.

Torney-Purta, J., R. Lehmann, H. Oswald, and W. Schulz. 2001. *Citizenship and Education in Twenty-Eight Countries: Civic Knowledge and Engagement at Age Fourteen*. Delft: IEA.

UNESCO. 1998a. *Citizenship Education for the 21st Century*. Paris: UNESCO.

UNESCO. 1998b. *Learning to Live Together in Peace and Harmony: Values Education for Peace, Human Rights, Democracy and Sustainable Development for the Asia-Pacific Region, a UNESCO-APNIEVE Source Book for Teacher Education and Tertiary Level Education.* Bangkok: UNESCO.

UNESCO. 2002. *Learning to Be: A Holistic and Integrated Approach to Values Education for Human Development: Core Values and the Valuing Process for Developing Innovative Practices for Values Education toward International Understanding and a Culture of Peace.* Bangkok: UNESCO.

UNESCO. 2011. *The Hidden Crisis: Armed Conflict and Education, Education for All Global Monitoring Report 2011.* Paris: UNESCO.

UNICEF. 2011. *The Role of Education in Peacebuilding: Literature Review.* New York: United Nations Children's Fund.

USAID. 2002. *Approaches to Civic Education: Lessons Learned.* Washington, DC: United States Agency for International Development (USAID).

Vriens, L. 2003. "Education for Peace: Concepts, Contexts and Challenges." In *Education of Minorities and Peace Education in Pluralistic Societies*, edited by Y. Iram and H. Wahrman, 57–74. Westport, CT: Praeger.

Wang, Z. 2009. "Old Wounds, New Narratives: Joint History Textbook Writing and Peacebuilding in East Asia." *History & Memory* 21 (1): 101–126.

Wessels, M. G. 2013. "Cosmology, Context, and Peace Education: A View from War Zones." In *Critical Peace Education: Difficult Dialogues*, edited by P. P. Trifonas and B. Wright, 89–104. New York: Springer.

Contextual and pedagogical considerations in teaching for forgiveness in the Arab world

Ilham Nasser[a], Mohammed Abu-Nimer[b] and Ola Mahmoud[a]

[a]*College of Education and Human Development, George Mason University, Fairfax, VA, USA;* [b]*School of International Service, American University, Washington, DC, USA*

> This study was conducted among Arab teachers in four countries in the Middle East (Jordan, Lebanon, Egypt and Palestine) to examine their views and methods on teaching for forgiveness in their classrooms. A total of 87 teachers in K-12 classrooms participated in semi-structured interviews as part of a larger study on teaching for forgiveness in the region. Thematic analyses of interviews suggested that teachers created opportunities to model and teach forgiveness as part of their civics education curriculum. They also expressed eagerness for instructional guidance and curriculum materials to systematically teach forgiveness in schools. The strength of religion and historical religious figures as positive sources for teaching forgiveness was also evident. Findings highlight the need to integrate education for peace and forgiveness in the education system, especially as a result of recent political developments in the Middle East, and to provide methods to assist teachers to do so in their classrooms.

1. Introduction

Studies on forgiveness are part of an emerging field of peace building.[1] The attitudes and beliefs people hold about forgiveness have been addressed by different disciplines such as religious studies, character education, social psychology, philosophy and conflict resolution (Zembylas and Michaelidou 2011). However, few empirical studies focused on forgiveness among individuals in conflict areas, particularly those in the Middle East. Of particular interest are teachers who might teach the topic as part of civics education and not necessarily religious studies, a content that is common in schools in Arab countries. The same scarcity exists when examining people's understanding of forgiveness and their related behaviours and actions.

This study is the first in the mentioned context to examine teachers' understanding and methods to teach for forgiveness. In the current conditions of unrest in the area, teachers can have a significant impact on students and communities. They serve as change agents for social change and transforming people's attitudes towards others. Thus, the main questions in this study focus on how Arab teachers view the importance of educating for forgiveness and how, if at all, they teach it in their classrooms; the necessary skills and tools Arab teachers utilise and need in order to engage in such a process; and in what situations do Arab teachers personally choose to forgive and the obstacles they face. This article is not focused on the macro level of political violence in Arab societies, however it does examine the potential roles that educators may play in addressing forgiveness on the macro and micro levels in schools.

2. Theoretical framework

Teachers play an important role as agents for positive change. From early childhood, school experiences can be critical in shaping students' self-esteem and developing social skills necessary to function as successful adults (Boulter 2004). Research suggests that incorporating positive values and building relationships with a teacher are essential in preventing violence among youth (Shumow and Miller 2001; Smith and Sandhu 2004; Maio et al. 2008). Educators have the potential to play a crucial role in building a culture of peace, especially in deeply divided societies that experience ongoing conflicts (Abu-Nimer 2000; Davies 2010). Education for forgiveness can be utilised to prepare students for encounters with the 'other' and for reducing stereotypes (Hewstone and Brown 1986; Abu-Nimer 1999). However, teaching for forgiveness is not the only solution for social and political ills but an important step to achieve more peaceful communities. Furthermore, this shouldn't imply that by teaching forgiveness, we can achieve social and political justice in the Arab world, but it is one of many interventions that need to be introduced in order to address the structural, social, political and psychological conditions and inequities existing in Arab societies.

Teachers' understanding of forgiveness in moral, political and social contexts affects what and how they teach and model forgiveness in their classrooms (Zembylas and Michaelidou 2011). Boulding (2000) emphasised the need to introduce education for peace (including forgiveness and reconciliation) as an integral component of every educational system and as a necessary step to prevent all forms of violence institutionally. Although educators are asked to address forgiveness and teach children to apologise for wrongdoing, many lack the proper pedagogy crucial to teach it (Lickona 1992). A main objective of this research is to determine critical components and skills needed for constructing forgiveness curricula.

Examining forgiveness from a critical pedagogy perspective, where education is more than transfer of knowledge but an affective investment in the learning process (Freire 1999; Giroux 2004), justifies a deeper investment in teaching for forgiveness. Based on the Freirian dialogic approach to creating social change, teachers can play a role when they change because 'the pedagogy and thus the liberation, is based on praxis: reflection and action upon the world in order to transform it' (Kent 1977, 37). Teachers have the power to raise awareness ('Conscientization', according to Freire) of the need for change and, as a result, increase engagement in learning and advocacy in ways that will and may transfer values, which Kent called 'Altering values' (39).

Exploring the best ways to assist teachers in creating those spaces for dialogue and raising awareness on forgiveness will contribute to our understanding of ways to change teachers and students' behaviours. According to Giroux (2004), 'Not only do students need to understand the ideological, economic, and political interests that shape the nature of their educational experiences, they must also address the strong emotional investments they may bring to such beliefs' (44). In Palestine, for example, Affouneh (2007) found that because of the unstable environments both inside and outside schools, Palestinian children displayed violent and dismissive attitudes and suffered from emotional and behavioural problems. This continued negative modelling generates negative outcomes in the form of psychological damage (i.e., violence towards others, post-traumatic stress disorders, bullying, panic attacks, self-withdrawal and muteness). Teachers have the ability to transform students and create better environments to challenge the status quo.

There is no consensus among researchers on one set definition for forgiveness (Ahmed and Braithwaite 2005; Chubbuck 2009; Zembylas and Michaelidou 2011; Zembylas 2012). Researchers, however, agree that forgiveness – although interconnected – should not be confused with reconciliation, pardoning or forgetting (Enright and Gassin 1992; Abu-Nimer 2008; Chubbuck 2009; Enright 2011; Zembylas and Michaelidou 2011). Reconciliation entails the broader long-term emotional and psychological aspects of a socio-cultural negotiation in which two or more parties work towards developing new emotions and beliefs that include coexistence and respect (Bar-Tal 2000; Hamber 2007; Enright 2011). Forgiveness, on the other hand, is the *moral* virtue that originates from within the self and is not dependent on accidental external situations for its expression (Enright 2011). Generally, forgiveness is defined in terms of decreasing the possible negative consequences of not forgiving, such as anger, retaliation and bitterness towards the aggressor, and instead increasing positive emotional and cognitive elements, including empathy, compassion and goodwill (Al-Mabuk, Enright, and Cardis 1995; APA 2006; Chubbuck 2009). Maio et al. (2008) define forgiveness as, 'a deliberate process that transforms a vengeful, negative response into a positive one' (307). Forgiveness is also defined as a, 'willingness to abandon one's right to resentment, negative judgment, and indifferent behavior toward one who unjustly hurt us, while fostering the undeserved qualities of compassion, generosity, and even love towards him or her' (Enright and Gassin 1992, 102). Scholars maintain that forgiveness is an act of ideally unconditional mercy and that it can occur independently of the wrongdoer expressing any remorse or apology. It is a complex mixture of emotional, cognitive and physical components (Denham et al. 2005).

Forgiveness is subjective and is understood differently depending on culture, interpersonal and intrapersonal relationships and dynamics, and context (Malcolm and Ramsey 2006). While interpersonal forgiveness is a process that occurs between two individuals on a private level, in which only the victim has the right to exercise forgiveness, intergroup forgiveness describes sociopolitical contexts in which defined groups are in conflict and require collective forgiveness in order for feuding sides to eventually trust each other (Hewstone et al. 2004; McLernon et al. 2004; Kadiangandu and Mullet 2007; Chubbuck 2009; Coen et al. 2010; Zembylas and Michaelidou 2011).

One of the most defining aspects of culture is religion. Papastephanou (2003) describes four types of forgiveness patterns most common in the Abrahamic traditions of Judaism, Christianity, and Islam: (1) forgiveness after punishment, (2) forgiveness without punishment, (3) unconditional forgiveness and (4) forgiveness and *a priori* culpability. These patterns reinforce the theory of context-dependency, which makes it difficult to categorise when forgiveness is possible or impossible, morally necessary or generous, or conditional (Papastephanou 2003). In Northern Ireland, Moeschberger et al. (2005) found an insignificant relationship between religious affiliation and intergroup forgiveness. This is largely consistent with the literature in both interpersonal (Gorsuch and Hao 1993) and intergroup (McLernon et al. 2004) settings.

In the context of the Middle East, this study assumes that educating and creating dialogues about forgiveness on the personal levels can contribute to the aspirations and potential to create societal, cultural and religious dialogues essential in promoting physical, cultural, religious and societal wellbeing, especially for the younger generations in these countries that are leading the move for political and social change – a transformative process that emerged and cannot be reversed. To move forward in a positive manner, teachers and their students have to 'invent and to find new social structures and new courses of action' to achieve more peaceful transformation (Kent 1977, 39). In addition, the discussion of forgiveness in this context mainly focuses on interpersonal and intra-community conflicts that take place and manifest in schools. Nevertheless, the macro political and communal violence cannot be ignored by teachers. Therefore, we assume that by introducing the concept of forgiveness and reconciliation in Arab schools' settings as a framework to reduce internal violence, teachers and students will be better prepared to respond and handle political violence.

3. Arab education systems: basic contextual features

Further understanding of the Arab educational systems, especially basic capacities of teachers, existing professional developments and overall challenges facing teachers engaged in civic education, might assist in appreciating the uniqueness of this research on forgiveness. Arab teachers face challenges in introducing social science topics in their schools. There are many reports that document the dire conditions of Arab education systems. According to the latest report, the entire Arab world significantly lags behind western countries, which is mainly explained when examining the low percentage of public spending on education from governments' overall expenditure[2].

In addition, researchers have linked the current revolts in Arab countries with the failure of their education systems to provide for the basic needs of youth. According to Watkins (2011, 2):

> Schools and universities are turning out graduates lacking the skills they need to succeed in employment markets, and the employment market itself is hamstrung by economic mismanagement. The result is high levels of education with mass unemployment.

The lack of professional and educational training for teachers and the lack of educational programmes that focus on diversity, critical thinking and conflict resolution are integral parts of the failure of the Arab education system. In a more specific survey of Arab education systems, teachers' preparation, climate and citizenship skills, Faour (2012, 6) concludes that:

> Unfortunately, in much of the Arab world school climates are generally negative. Many students do not feel safe physically, socially, and emotionally in schools. Substantial percentages of teachers entered their profession with deficient academic preparation and pre-service training and do not receive adequate and appropriate professional development during service.

Faour (2012) also adds that most students from 4th and 8th grade from the Arab countries scored below the international average on Trends in International Mathematics and Science Study (TIMSS). He continues that physical punishment and other forms of violence such as bullying are part of the daily experience of many students in the Arab schools.

A similar reality was documented regarding teachers' preparation, in which the majority of the teachers are underprepared and lack proper academic degrees to teach their subject matter (especially in Mathematics). Such a reality of lack of preparation and qualification is more prevalent in the lower grades. For example, of 11 Arab countries with data on preschool teachers, only 5 countries had all their teachers trained. At the primary school level, of 12 countries with data, only 7 countries had all their teachers trained. At the secondary level, of six countries with data, only three countries had all their teachers trained. In general, according to the index of school climate in the Arab countries all the countries, except Lebanon and Dubai (in United Arab Emirates), had negative index values, indicating an overall negative school climate (UNESCO 2010).[3]

The above brief review illustrates the need to increase formal and informal educational programmes that focus on skills and values that support self-confidence, problem solving, non-violence and forgiveness and reconciliation. Thus, our proposed research is to examine the current perceptions of Arab teachers regarding these concepts in order to enhance their capacity to address such challenges in their educational environments and, as a result, view themselves as agents for critical pedagogy and transformative education.

4. Methods and techniques

Semi-structured interviews were conducted to collect teachers' views about teaching for forgiveness. Teachers who volunteered were part of a larger study that aimed to survey teachers' attitudes towards hypothetical forgiveness situations and their reasoning behind forgiving or not. The researchers followed a snowball methodology to reach volunteers. The interview protocol was developed in English and went through multiple translations into Arabic to ensure accuracy in content and understanding. Four field researchers, who collected the survey data and were natives of each country, conducted the interviews, which lasted between 30 and 40 minutes each.

A qualitative approach was selected to elicit teachers' responses on forgiveness because it provides the participants with opportunities to share in person (face to face) and in depth perspectives about the topic. Also, individual interviews were used to provide participants with a private and comfortable space to express their views and opinions (Bloom et al. 2001). It was especially critical to convey this message to participants because of teachers' reluctance to voice their opinions. There is also a common mistrust of research in Arab communities, especially during the social and political unrest in several countries in the region. This required some flexibility on the researchers' part and resulted in the audiotaping of some interviews and researchers' notes or notes written by the participants themselves[4] on others.

In interviews, open-ended questions were used and these were: 'What do you teach to addresses the value of forgiveness in your classroom?', 'How do you teach for forgiveness to your students?', 'Does your curriculum address and deal with forgiveness and how?', 'What motivates you to forgive?', 'Who is a role model that can be a symbol or example of forgiveness in your community?' and 'What would prevent you personally from forgiving and in what situations?' Key concept analysis was utilised (Krueger 1998; Krueger and Anne 2009) when two researchers separately read the interviews and generated dominant themes for each of the questions and together decided on a list of common themes, compiled the frequency of emerging themes, followed by a third researcher reviewing the data again and confirming main themes.

4.1. Participants

Participants in this study were teachers from schools and regions in the four countries. A total of 87 teachers of different grade levels and living arrangements (rural and urban) were interviewed (26 from Egypt, 21 from Jordan, 20 from Lebanon, and 20 from Palestine (West Bank)).[5] We were able to collect demographic information on participants from all except for Palestine. Participants were similar in that all but two had university degrees, their mean age was 31, half were married and half single and most of them were Muslims (except for seven Christians and two Druze).[6] Participants were also asked about the importance of religion as indicated on a Likert scale (1 = not important at all, 2 = not important, 3 = of some importance, 4 = important and 5 = very important). Responses suggest religion was important or very important for all participants from Egypt and most of the participants from Jordan. In Lebanon, about half of the participants believed religion was important or very important. The rest thought religion was moderately important (seven) or not important at all. Despite the fact that we lack data on importance of religion for Palestinian participants, one can safely say, based on the interviews, that religion was important for most of the teachers.

5. Results

The qualitative analysis of interviews generated main themes that were important across countries and religions. The following presents emerging themes that were in common amongst teachers.

5.1. The need to teach for forgiveness

Teachers interviewed agreed it is possible to teach for forgiveness as part of their existing curriculum and that they attempt to teach it. However, they do not have a concrete, systematic and unified curriculum or methodology on how to introduce it. Thus social and religious studies were the primary formal curriculum identified as possible venues. All emphasised that there is a pressing need to teach forgiveness in Arab schools, especially with the rising forms of social violence penetrating the schools and higher education institutes. In addition, they agreed there are limited methods and techniques on how to introduce the concept. Despite this challenge, some Arab teachers are taking the notion of teaching forgiveness into their own hands. A Palestinian teacher elaborated on that and detailed examples of violence as one of the most pressing issues in schools: 'As a teacher, I notice the influence of TV on small children starting from 5th grade how they hit each other, they are easily influenced by violence and the video games they play.' The participant continued:

> So for example there are a lot of problems between students who support the football teams 'Real Madrid' and 'Barcelona', so I created a play to try to heal this phenomenon. So I told them instead of fighting we come up with clubs to create ideas – anything great started with an idea.

The above illustrates how teachers address situations requiring their intervention and their methods in dealing with daily conflicts. It also illustrates the common belief that violence is imported from Western media and that there is a need to combat that. Nevertheless, Arab teachers are forced to deal with the dominance of various Western trends (values and norms affiliated with new technology, social media and other cultural exports) and their impact on students' behaviours in their classroom.

The above example also responds to the frustration among teachers that values are theoretically introduced to students without any practical ways to apply them. As stated by a Palestinian teacher: 'What I ask is that teaching of values should be both theoretical and practical so that [it] reaches student in a way that they can apply it in their community.'

5.2. *Forgiveness in formal curriculum*

In the four countries there is no formal and intentionally designed curriculum that directly deals with teaching for forgiveness. Participants were clear that they have no specific books or guidelines on how to introduce forgiveness in their classrooms. However, many confirmed that there are (usually popular) stories in history, Islamic studies and social studies that are used by teachers to disseminate the value of forgiveness. Furthermore, an overwhelming majority of the teachers supported the need to design curriculum modules on forgiveness in their schools. They expressed eagerness to teach it and articulated the benefits of educating their students for forgiveness. It should be noted that some teachers argued that forgiveness cannot be a special theme to be taught based on a text. According to one teacher from Lebanon:

> Forgiveness is a culture that you disseminate. It is a choice you make as a teacher or school. There is no Chapter 3 on 'Forgiveness in Schools'. It is a value which you as a teacher have the choice to spread.

However, for many teachers the concept and practice of forgiveness in the context of the school constituted a challenge that can affect the students' capacity to learn responsibility. In the mind of teachers, if forgiveness means an educator does not discipline the students for their mistakes or negligence, it will lead to further irresponsible behaviour. Punishment and disciplinary actions taken by the teachers were thus seen as necessary. According to a Lebanese teacher, 'Students shouldn't be held accountable for trivial mistakes because this can result in dismissal from school.' The teacher continues:

> How can a student learn about forgiveness if we do not apply it? At the same time, how can we forgive students for behaviours that may become bigger problems in the future? We have no balance between these two positions. Forgiving students for small mistakes can also contribute to their becoming irresponsible.

The examples above illustrate that teachers see forgiveness as a matter dealt with on the interpersonal level. It is a problem between one student and another or a student and a teacher and not one that is dealt with on the community or intergroup levels. It is apparent that teachers chose that because of the plethora of issues they face daily. For some teachers, forgiveness is partly based on maintaining control over their classrooms. Here, forgiveness is not about forgetting or condoning offences, which indicates a tension between the desire to teach for forgiveness without expecting rewards and keeping one's rights and justice. In addition, teachers' perceptions of forgiveness collided with their perceptions and need to follow the schools' regulations and rules. Forgiveness does not necessarily contradict the need to enforce laws and seek justice.

5.3. Forgiveness pedagogy

Teachers named various methods used to teach forgiveness such as guidance and mediation (43 teachers), modelling (30), student-centred activities (22), teaching values (40) and direct instruction (36). Teachers inerviewed shared examples and suggested strategies they use to teach forgiveness when students violate school regulations, miss homework, engage in violence and so on. A Jordanian teacher explained about guidance: 'I listen to both sides of the problem; we discuss the issue, and continue to dialogue till we get to forgiveness and end the problem.'

In addition, teachers saw the importance and need for role models as a way to display positive behaviours to students. As one Jordanian teacher said: 'We teachers should be role models and forgive students when they make mistakes and not seek revenge and be angry with a misbehaving student.' Another Palestinian teacher added: 'I am a human being with feelings but that doesn't mean I behave as I wish. A teacher has to always be forgiving and act as a role model to students in every word, behavior, and situation.'

Teachers, especially in Jordan and Lebanon, highlighted student-centred activities such as songs, stories, poems and other activities to promote, model and teach examples of forgiveness. In addition, cooperative learning such as role-play and group work was also described as tools to internalise forgiveness. This is an interesting approach to teaching and learning that goes against the traditional teacher-centred teaching in many Arab schools. It is encouraging to see that teachers understood the value of child-centred pedagogy and highlighted that in interviews. Nevertheless, it is possible that teachers provided desirable responses to our research team but they might have sincerely been trained in more innovative approaches to teaching. It might also be due to the fact that teachers were relatively young and as a result might be more trained and open to using such student-centred methods.

5.4. *Motivation to forgive*

The question on motivations was apparently difficult in terms of defining teachers' perceptions of forgiveness. They questioned the moral arguments they can make to encourage forgiveness among students. For example, a Palestinian teacher explained how to justify forgiveness behaviour among students:

> We ask our students what does it mean that your classmate hit you, and that you are bleeding, in the future your classmate may stand by you during difficult times, don't ever insult anyone for you may need him in the future, for a problem, or money and you will find him standing by you, and that is why forgiveness needs to be between students.

This teacher conveys the potential gains from forgiveness to his students.

Overall, several major categories emerged when asked about motivations for forgiveness. Teachers highlighted motivations related to their faith and religious teachings (50 teachers out of 87), social harmony, love and peace (33), empathy and human nature (16) and culture/traditions (11). The importance of faith, religion and religious teaching as a resource and incentive (rewards, God forgives, reward in heaven) for people to be forgiving and to teach forgiveness is highly motivating for teachers here – a recurrent theme amongst both Muslim and Christian participants. A majority of teachers (lowest in Lebanon) highlighted stories from the Quran and the New Testament as their preferred methods to convey forgiveness messages to their students. An Egyptian teacher explained the necessary link between forgiveness and religion in education when he was asked about the national curriculum and to what extent it incorporates forgiveness:

> The school curriculum contains very little about forgiveness, but it needs a change in the style and emphasis of presentation of values and that cannot happen without connecting the kids with their religion, because it teaches them forgiveness and pardoning. We are nations [Arabs] who only respond to religion.

This emphasis on the importance of religion to Arabs is relevant because the teacher is urging schools to use religion as a springboard to teach forgiveness, a topic that certainly is well received by students, families and communities. In such a context of sacredness of religious sources, it is rare that anyone disputes constructive or inclusive religious teachings. Thus, teachers can utilise forgiveness through religion without opposition from the community. On the contrary, such values or approach will be supported, as stated above.

Similarly, when asked about the most important sources for forgiveness in her/his society, an Egyptian interviewee responded: 'Religion, because the Egyptian people are religious by nature and cannot accept things that go against their religious beliefs.' Such links to the teachers' faith and religion were made not only among Muslims, but Christian teachers as well. An Egyptian Christian teacher cited the story of Pope John Paul II 'forgiving his would-be assassin'. Another Christian teacher cited Christ on the cross as a powerful example of forgiveness and recited biblical justifications for the need to forgive, for example: 'for if you forgive men when they sin against you, your heavenly Father will also forgive you' (Matthew 6:14).

An additional theme that emerged as a motivation to teach forgiveness was empathy and human nature (empathy was used in the context of the tendency to empathise with people who make mistakes). Teachers, especially in Lebanon, emphasised that, when teaching, it is important to stress empathy with the person committing the wrongdoing. Their rationale for such emphasis was related to their views of two elements: it is 'human nature to commit mistakes' and the 'lack of intentionality'. As one Lebanese teacher elaborated: 'I try to remain positive and think that the other person wronged me unintentionally.'

Consistent references to love, peace and harmony, by 33 of the 87 teachers, indicated that they are motivated to teach for forgiveness because it is much needed to create and maintain a peaceful and united society. One Palestinian teacher explained, 'Thus, in addition to teaching historic and religious events, teachers need to use their influential roles to stress these values in their schools.' Another added that it is necessary to teach forgiveness because, 'Forgiveness is nice; it leads to love, harmony, and cooperation in the community.' Nevertheless, according to participating teachers, for forgiveness education in schools to be effective, there is a need to use everyday events and interactions to teach forgiveness. Such an assertion is challenging in many Arab communities, like Jordanian, Egyptian, Lebanese and Palestinian contexts, because of the lack of systematic educational curricula to address or engage in this topic because in most of these contexts, peace education is not an integral part of the existing national curriculum.

5.5. *Forgiveness figures and symbols*

When asked who can be a major figure and symbol for forgiveness, teachers highlighted the role of family (especially parents) and the immediate community as examples, references and sources. Many teachers also strongly voiced (again based on a count of frequent mention of themes) the view that elders in the family play an integral role in modelling forgiveness and that religious leadership (clergy, priests and scholars) are expected and ought to play the same role. In addition, teachers saw themselves as symbols and spoke repeatedly about current examples of forgiveness figures in their respective communities.

All participants, regardless of country of origin, emphasised the crucial role their parents had in educating for forgiveness in their lives. Many teachers managed to identify a family member, neighbour or friend as an example of forgiveness. Many of them even shared concrete examples of situations in which these figures exercised forgiveness. Parenthood, especially motherhood, was elevated to the highest level among the teachers in their perception of the most forgiving figure that can be cited in their lives. Teachers provided several stories that they share with their students about the power of love and forgiveness that characterises the revered role of mothers in Arab culture. A famous Arabic story about a mother who sacrificed her 'heart' for her son was told by several teachers interviewed.

Although the social status of teachers in the Arab context has been deteriorating, many asserted that their students and people in general continue to perceive them as central figures and symbols in shaping children's values and beliefs. Thus, fostering the value of forgiveness in their work is accepted and even expected. Teachers said that teaching forgiveness at school involves the use of appropriate values (both social and religious) and examples (stories) in classroom discussions, modelling and mediating and guidance. They provided many specific examples of disciplinary practices they use in their classrooms that illustrate how forgiving they are. They also emphasised themselves as models for their students in that they try not to shout at, punish or disrespect students.

Furthermore, teachers identified historical religious leaders as role models for teaching forgiveness. Among Muslim participants, the Prophet was the main figure who needed to be emulated for his forgiving behaviour: 'We shouldn't forget that the best example for us is the Prophet. For the Prophet is always the best example for us to be guided by in little and big matters.' Even when teachers recognised their capacity to be a role model of forgiveness, a number of them repeated the need to follow the Prophet as the ultimate role model of Muslims. As one Palestinian teacher said:

> I teach the story of Abu Lahab and his wife; how they treated the Prophet, how his wife would carry the wood and throw it in front of his house, also how he would put rubbish in front of his house, and how the Prophet treated them with goodness instead and forgave them. This gives a very strong example of forgiveness. Our Prophet is the best role model for us and we have to follow his example.

When asked about a current leader or symbol for forgiveness, many teachers expressed the lack of living religious figures that are examples of forgiveness. A Palestinian teacher voiced this disappointment in current symbols and figures:

> I can't say there is anyone now except from the religious books. There are no messengers/prophets in the community so the situation is different. I can't apply or force something that happened over a thousand years ago now. I can take understandings but can't implement it to my 2nd grade class or my 15-year-old son, he would make fun of me and tell me that you want to apply something from a semi-perfect time to our community now that has a lot of problems. That doesn't work. We don't live in a perfect city, nor was there in history a perfect city, or someone will call me an idiot for forgiving in everything.

The above example illustrates teachers' views of themselves as going against mainstream thought when attempting to educate for forgiveness. There is a mixture of realism and disappointment in the inability to be in a desired environment where people live in harmony. This disappointment was also expressed on the national level, where there was a consensus amongst teachers from the four countries that it is 'very rare to find a living public figure these days that is an example for forgiveness' in the Arab world. The overwhelming majority of teachers did not name any current figure as a role model for forgiveness. All teachers pointed out that the current leaders in their societies do not display any forgiving behaviour to be emulated. A Lebanese teacher elaborated, 'There is no leader in Lebanon who currently can be a role model for forgiveness. They are all liars and after revenge. There is no leader who can be a role model for me and for his people.'

There were few interviewees (four) who identified political figures as a role model for forgiveness. Such leaders are politically controversial and could even be seen as contradictory to the value or meaning of forgiveness. For example, one Palestinian teacher saw Yasser Arafat – known as Abu Ammar (the former leader of the Palestine Liberation Organisation) – as a symbol of forgiveness. He said:

> I am a Palestinian and love my country a lot. The great leader Abu Ammar was the height of forgiveness for everyone; and me during his life he didn't

give up and was always strong, pushing problems away from us. Personally, it is my father, God blesses him, and since my childhood he taught me the concept of forgiveness.

The lack of most teachers' connection to forgiving Arab public figures is an indicator of several challenges facing Arab communities such as the internal and external conflicts and instability, lack of media attention to the whole notion of reconciliation or to positive social trends and the discourse on forgiveness being still largely confined to religious historical events and figures.

Teaching forgiveness cannot be left to teachers' own individual and personal perceptions. The need for a systematised approach and even an agreed-upon set of definitions and examples is also reflected in the type of illustrations that another teacher from Egypt cited as examples in their societies. The teacher said, 'Al Azhar [a major mosque and university in Egypt] is a symbol of forgiveness because it holds dialogue with all religions and accepts them and highlights the good qualities of Islam.'

The quote above illustrates teachers' ability and desire to move the conversation from the interpersonal and school-related levels to the more intergroup and public levels where there exists a need for teachings for forgiveness such as in the case of interreligious dialogue.

The results reveal trends in teachers' ideas about what and how to teach for forgiveness. They also shed light on teachers' values of themselves and their roles as well as using the resources available to them as a way to approach this difficult topic. They used religion, traditions and historic events to address the topic in their classrooms.

6. Discussion and implications

In examining the results of this study, it appears that they are partially confirming the assumptions we made, especially about teachers' eagerness to teach for forgiveness and the timing of teaching such a theme in Arab society which is going through rapid social and political changes. The results provide an in-depth view of the complexities of teachers' ideas, their teaching practices and their conflicting views regarding teaching for forgiveness. For example, it was expected that teachers would utilise religion in their responses, which was confirmed in the interviews. This result is also supported by previous research conducted by two of the authors (Nasser and Abu-Nimer 2012), suggesting that religious discourse in Arab society is essential in conceptualising and understanding the concept of forgiveness and reconciliation in the Arab cultural context. Nevertheless, despite the importance of religious teaching and figures in their lives and as a source for forgiveness teaching, participants sought current, less traditional or religiously based forgiving practices to share with students.

Teachers were also eager to utilise new and up-to-date ideas, practices and strategies to teach for forgiveness. Complicating their readiness to relate forgiveness to the modern societies they lived in, was that they could not identify with current religious or political figures who are models for teaching and practising forgiveness and who can function as messengers or symbols that Arab teachers can be proud of. This eagerness stems from the lack of proper preparation and professional development opportunities for Arab teachers in general. This notion is supported by Faour's (2012) report on teachers in Arab countries where the author discusses the low quality of teaching teams in Arab countries, low levels of preparation and lack of investment in professional development of teachers.

Despite the political unrest in some of the countries included in this study, especially in Egypt, Lebanon and Palestine, teachers expressed a positive outlook on forgiveness. Teachers were aware of the role the topic has in creating united and harmonious communities, even in Palestine where people live under harsh conditions of occupation. Palestinian participants emphasised the role of forgiveness in promoting social and familial peace. Teachers were also positive about the question of how to teach for forgiveness. The results also confirmed the findings of other scholars (Shumow and Miller 2001; Maio et al. 2008) regarding the crucial role that schools can play in the absence of other socialisation agencies. Teachers mentioned being role models and spoke of their responsibility in leading the young generation to become more forgiving. They also highlighted student-centred methods of teaching, such as cooperative learning techniques and role playing, as ways to teach the topic. Teachers interviewed appeared open to learning more about methods and techniques to teach for forgiveness, such as dialogic conversations and discussions, as in the Freirian pedagogy. They were eager to move beyond their need for immediate responses to discipline issues and to learn about the principles of communication, dialogue and cooperation. Based on the results, teachers were familiar enough with these techniques to name them all, but it is not clear to what extent these methods are being utilised. Observations in the classroom and follow ups with pupils are areas for further research.

Teachers had some confusion around the definition of forgiveness, when to forgive and where, and under what conditions. They agreed about the need to instil forgiveness in the curriculum, but they aligned forgiveness with other concepts. For example, tolerance, conflict resolution and reconciliation (all similar terms in Arabic, with similar roots) were used to describe situations of forgiveness. It should be noted that there were teachers who offered their own definition of forgiveness and explained that they use this personal understanding as a guiding principle when educating for forgiveness. For example, a Palestinian female teacher who teaches in an all-girls' school stated:

> We define forgiveness as doing good to those who wronged you. It is repaying wrongdoing with goodness. We teach this definition a lot to the girls in our school. The person who forgives is like a tree that had rocks thrown at her and gave fruits in return.

This trend of providing personal definitions only illustrates the wide range of understanding of the boundaries and nature of forgiveness. Some used leaders to describe them as symbols, such as Yasser Arafat (the late leader of the Palestine Liberation Organisation) and Al Azhar mosque in Egypt. Such variation is not unusual because in the literature there are multiple disciplines and views and theoretical and practical attempts to define the concept of forgiveness.

These personal definitions of forgiveness are consistent with the literature about the difficulty of defining forgiveness as it is subjective and based on many different factors, like religious beliefs, personality, context and others. Nevertheless, it is noticeable that in this study, teachers in general perceived forgiveness as a personal and individual rather than an intergroup act or activity. There were only few attempts to expand the definition beyond the school walls. The implications, here, mean we shouldn't leave the concept of forgiveness undefined for educators because it allows for too many definitions of the concept and takes away from its educational focus. Such a task can be highly problematic and challenging considering the political turmoil and ideological conflicts at play in the Arab world.

Furthermore, another important dilemma that was voiced by several teachers relates to the issue of accountability and justice when forgiving a student, especially when he or she violated schools' rules and regulations. As stated in the literature, the act of forgiveness by the victim does not necessarily imply that the offender will not face institutional or legal accountability (Rigby 2000; Henderson 2005). Thus, there is a differentiation between individual, collective and institutional forgiveness. For example, a teacher can forgive the student for breaking the rules, however such a decision will not imply that such student will not bear the responsibility of his/her mistake. Developing such complex understanding and differentiations between the various types and processes of forgiveness in social and educational settings often requires special intervention such as training programmes, special curricula and intentional preparations. The Arab education systems certainly do not have such opportunities. However, surprisingly, American and European educational systems also lack such specific programmes (Enright and Gassin 1992).

A major challenge that faces Arab teachers when introducing a pedagogy of forgiveness in their schools relates to the huge gap between their views of the early-historical period of Islam (the Prophet's and Companions' periods) and the current reality of the Arab and Muslim world. They all agreed that utilising the early period as a source for educating for forgiveness seemed ideal and necessary. Nevertheless, some voiced concerns that students may have serious doubts about the applicability of these values, norms and practices today. Such a challenge is typical to many social change agents in Muslim contexts in which there is a huge perceptional gap between the social and political reality and the internal Islamic religious discourse of peace, reconciliation and forgiveness. Thus, many participants in educational programmes and training workshops about peace and forgiveness often engage in the question of if the Islamic religious traditions are rich with such ideals, then how do we explain the reality of religious extremism, violence and conditions of social injustice in most of if not all the Arab countries (Abu-Nimer 2003). Overcoming this frustration and finding responses to explain this gap between desired images of the past and present reality requires awareness and professional capacity building in which teachers examine their own views about sources of current violence in their personal, political and social environments. Such opportunities for professional training and preparations were certainly identified as a pressing need among all teachers regardless of their age, gender or country of origin.

The results regarding the motivation to teach forgiveness as a tool to bring social harmony are also consistent with previous research about the practical aspects and implications of forgiveness behaviours. In Denham et al. (2005), the motivation to forgive is influenced by two different thoughts: (1) you forgive because of personal and practical gains that a person gets when forgiving, such as in the example of the teacher elaborating on how he explains to students the need to forgive because you might need the person you forgive in the future; and (2) you forgive regardless of the reward and as a virtue of being a good human being, or a good follower of your faith, as indicated by many of the teachers we interviewed. The latter is a much-needed objective in teaching for forgiveness in the Arab world in order to build a 'culture of peace', using Boulding's (2000) term. This motivation to forgive because you are a good human being is repeatedly expressed by teachers, using words such as love and harmony possibly as a method to counter the discourse and narratives of hatred, sectarianism and religious divisions prevalent in Arab societies these days.

Arab teachers in this study had a strong faith and belief in the role of immediate family and community, especially family elders (with emphasis on parents), as role models and examples for children in teaching for forgiveness. This is a very positive sign for educators who seek to plan intervention strategies on the topic. Participating teachers, especially from Jordan (six participants) cited the 'Urf' (tribal traditional dispute resolution) as a mechanism that can help facilitate forgiveness in the school context, especially if these processes are carried out according to the 'proper traditional values and procedures'. Obviously, the practice of Urf is widespread in Arab tribal and traditional communities, however it is not accepted or practised among urban middle- and upper-class sectors. In addition, it can be highly disputed in its value in contributing to forgiveness and reconciliation – several studies have documented its limitations (Irani and Funk 1998; Abu-Nimer 2003). Similarly, this result also confirmed existing conclusions in the literature on the importance of culture in practising and conceptualising forgiveness (Cehajic, Brown, and Castano 2008; Philpot and Hornsey 2010). Arab teachers' views on forgiveness were greatly affected by their cultural heritage, especially their religious traditions. It is clear though that there is agreement about the importance of teaching for forgiveness at all levels of schooling and an eagerness to be part of the design of curriculum materials on the topic.

Finally, this research is a contribution to the field of forgiveness studies because it increases our knowledge on forgiveness education in the Arab cultural and educational contexts. The research outcomes have implications for conflict interventions in Arab schools and communities and, more specifically, educators, who have a huge impact on their students and their beliefs and perceptions (Nasser and Abu-Nimer 2012). Some of these implications include the need to incorporate forgiveness in any future programmes on reconciliation and conflict resolution in educational settings, the need to pay special attention to the role of elders in the community when proposing new intervention programmes on forgiveness, and that both Islamic and Christian teachings on forgiveness are necessary sources to promote forgiveness. In addition, bridging the gap between the ideals and virtues (such as forgiveness, dialogue, peace and so on) presented to students based on religious teachings and the current social and political reality in the Arab societies is a major obstacle that needs to be addressed by any educational programme. The results of the study can guide professionals in peace education and curriculum design and instruction to construct a research-based, comprehensive curriculum on forgiveness. The results also provide directions on the next steps in the research and highlight the importance of studying other players such as students, family and community leaders and their views.

Funding

This work was supported by Kindle Foundation and Fetzer Foundation.

Notes

1. The authors use peace building as an umbrella term that includes several areas of studies such as peace education, conflict resolution and transformation and peace studies. Forgiveness and reconciliation are certainly integral parts of these areas.
2. Arab Human Development Report, data reflected for the years 2007 and 2008 (http://www.arab-hdr.org/data/indicators/2012-27.aspx).
3. The index included six criteria: Safety; Teachers' professional development on improving teaching skills in the two years that preceded the survey; Teachers'

Working Conditions; Students' learning methods; Learning resource; Parental involvement.
4. This was especially true in the case of Egypt, where teachers who refused to be audiotaped were provided with the written questions to write their responses to.
5. This area is still under Israeli occupation since 1967 and part of a proposed Palestinian state with Gaza.
6. Druze is a sect of Islam.

References

Abu-Nimer, M. 1999. *Conflict Resolution and Change. Arab–Jewish Encounters in Israel*. New York, NY: SUNY Press.
Abu-Nimer, M. 2000. "Peace-Building in Post Settlement: Challenges for Israeli and Palestinian Peace Education." *Peace and Conflict: Journal of Peace Psychology* 6 (1): 1–21.
Abu-Nimer, M. 2003. *Nonviolence and Peace-Building in Islamic Context*. University of Florida.
Abu-Nimer, M. 2008. "The Role of Religious Peacebuilding in Traumatized Societies: From Withdrawal to Forgiveness." In *Peacebuilding in Traumatized Societies*, edited by B. Hart, 239–261. New York: University Press of America.
Affouneh, S. J. 2007. "How Sustained Conflict Makes Moral Education Impossible: Some Observations from Palestine." *Journal of Moral Education* 36 (3): 343–356.
Ahmed, E., and J. Braithwaite. 2005. "Forgiveness, Shaming, Shame and Bullying." *The Australian and New Zealand Journal of Criminology* 38 (3): 298–323.
Al-Mabuk, R., R. D. Enright, and P. Cardis. 1995. "Forgiveness Education with Parentally Love-Deprived College Students." *Journal of Moral Education* 24 (4): 427–444.
American Psychological Association. 2006. *Forgiveness: A Sampling of Research Results*. Washington, DC: Office of International Affairs. Reprinted 2008.
Bar-Tal, D. 2000. "From Intractable Conflict through Conflict Resolution to Reconciliation: Psychological Analysis." *Political Psychology* 21 (2): 351–365.
Bloom, M., J. Frankland, M. Thomas, and K. Robson. 2001. *Focus Groups in Social Research*. Thousand Oaks, CA: Sage.
Boulding, E. 2000. *Culture of Peace: The Hidden Side of History*. Syracuse, NY: Syracuse University Press.
Boulter, L. 2004. "Family-School Connection and School Violence Prevention." *The Negro Educational Review* 55 (1): 27–40.
Cehajic, S., R. Brown, and E. Castano. 2008. "Forgive and Forget? Antecedents and Consequences of Intergroup Forgiveness in Bosnia and Herzegovina." *Political Psychology* 29 (3): 351–367.
Chubbuck, S. 2009. "Forgiveness Education: Urban Youth's Perceptions and Collective Narratives." *Journal for the Study of Peace and Conflict* 2009–2010: 77–88.
Coen, S., M. Noor, R. J. Brown, L. Taggert, and A. Fernandez. 2010. "Intergroup Identity Perceptions and Their Implications for Intergroup Forgiveness: The Common Ingroup Identity Model and Its Efficacy in the Field." *Irish Journal of Psychology* 31 (3): 151–170.

Davies, L. 2010. "The Different Faces of Education in Conflict." *Development* 53 (4): 491–497.
Denham, S., K. Neal, B. Wilson, K. Pickering, and C. J. Boyatzis. 2005. "Emotional Development and Forgiveness in Children: Emerging Evidence." In *Handbook of Forgiveness*, edited by E. L. Worthington, 127–139. New York, NY: Routledge.
Enright, R. D. 2011. *Psychological Science of Forgiveness: Implications for Psychotherapy and Education*. Rome, Italy: Neuroscienza e Azione Morale.
Enright, R., and E. Gassin. 1992. "Forgiveness: A Developmental View." *Journal of Moral Education* 21 (2): 99–114.
Faour, M. 2012. *Arab World's Education Report Card: School Climate and Citizenship Skills*. Washington, DC: Carnegie Middle East Center.
Freire, P. 1999. *Pedagogy of Freedom*. Lanham, MD: Rowman & Littlefield.
Giroux, F. 2004. "Critical Pedagogy and the Postmodern/Modern Divide: Towards a Pedagogy of Democratization." *Teacher Education Quarterly* 31 (1): 31–47.
Gorsuch, R., and J. Hao. 1993. "Forgiveness: An Exploratory Factor Analysis and Its Relationships to Religious Variables." *Review of Religious Research* 34 (4): 333–347.
Hamber, B. 2007. "Forgiveness and Reconciliation: Paradise Lost or Pragmatism?" *Peace & Conflict: Journal of Peace Psychology* 13 (1): 115–125.
Henderson, M. 2005. *Forgiveness: Breaking the Chain of Hate*. Portland, OR: Arnica Publishing.
Hewstone, M., and R. Brown, eds. 1986. *Control and Conflict in Intergroup Encounters*. Oxford: Basil Blackwell.
Hewstone, M., E. Cairns, A. Voci, F. McLernon, U. Niens, and M. Noor. 2004. "Intergroup Forgiveness and Guilt in Northern Ireland: Social Psychological Dimensions of 'the Troubles'." In *Collective Guilt: International Perspectives*, edited by N. R. Branscombe and B. Doosje, 193–215. New York: Cambridge University Press.
Irani, G. E., and N. C. Funk. 1998. "Rituals of Reconciliation: Arab Islamic Perspectives." *Arab Studies Quarterly* 20 (4): 53–73.
Kadiangandu, J. K., and E. Mullet. 2007. "Intergroup Forgiveness: A Congolese Perspective." *Peace and Conflict: Journal of Peace Psychology* 13 (1): 37–49.
Kent, G. 1977. "Peace Education: Pedagogy of the Middle Class." *Peace and Change* IV (3): 37–42.
Krueger, R. 1998. *Analyzing and Reporting Focus Group Results*. Thousand Oaks, CA: Sage.
Krueger, R. C., and M. Anne. 2009. *Focus Groups: A Practical Guide for Applied Research*. 4th ed. Thousand Oaks, CA: Sage.
Lickona, T. 1992. *Educating for Character: How Our Schools Can Teach Respect and Responsibility*. New York, NY: Bantam.
Maio, G., G. Thomas, F. Fincham, and K. Carnelley. 2008. "Unraveling the Role of Forgiveness in Family Relationships." *Journal of Personality and Social Psychology* 94 (2): 307–319.
Malcolm, L., and J. Ramsey. 2006. "Teaching and Learning Forgiveness: A Multi-dimensional Approach." *Teaching Theology & Religion* 9 (3): 175–185. doi:10.1111/j.1467-9647.2006.00281.x
McLernon, F., E. Cairns, M. Hewstone, and R. Smith. 2004. "The Development of Intergroup Forgiveness in Northern Ireland." *Journal of Social Issues* 60 (3): 587–601.

Moeschberger, S. L., D. N. Dixon, U. Niens, and E. Cairns. 2005. "Forgiveness in Northern Ireland: Model for Peace in the Midst of the 'Troubles'." *Peace and Conflict: Journal of Peace Psychology* 11 (2): 199–214.

Nasser, I., and M. Abu-Nimer. 2012. "Perceptions of Forgiveness among Palestinian Teachers in Israel." *Journal of Peace Education* 9 (1): 1–15.

Papastephanou, M. 2003. "Forgiving and Requesting Forgiveness." *Journal of Philosophy of Education* 37 (3): 503–524.

Philpot, C. R., and M. J. Hornsey. 2010. "Memory for Intergroup Apologies and Its Relationship with Forgiveness." *European Journal of Social Psychology* 41 (1): 96–106.

Rigby, A. 2000. *Justice and Reconciliation after the Violence*. Boulder, CO: Lynne Rienner.

Shumow, L., and J. Miller. 2001. "Parents' At-Home and At-School Academic Involvement with Young Adolescents.." *Journal of Early Adolescence* 21 (1): 68–91.

Smith, D., and D. Sandhu. 2004. "Toward a Positive Perspective on Violence Prevention in Schools: Building Connections." *Journal of Counseling and Development* 82 (3): 287–293.

UNESCO. 2010. Institute for Statistics, Global Education Digest 2010. Comparing Education Statistics across the World (Arabic version), Tables 1, 3, and 6.

Watkins, K. 2011. Education Failures Fan the Flames in the Arab World. *Education for All Global Monitoring Report*. Accessed September 12, 2013. http://efareport.wordpress.com/2011/02/23/education-failures-fan-the-flames-in-the-Arab-world/

Zembylas, M. 2012. "Teaching about/for Ambivalent Forgiveness in Troubled Societies." *Ethics and Education* 7 (1): 19–32.

Zembylas, M., and A. Michaelidou. 2011. "Teachers' Understandings of Forgiveness in a Troubled Society: An Empirical Exploration and Implications for Forgiveness Pedagogies." *Pedagogies: An International Journal* 6 (3): 250–264.

Global citizenship as education for peacebuilding in a divided society: structural and contextual constraints on the development of critical dialogic discourse in schools

Jacqueline Reilly[a] and Ulrike Niens[b]

[a]School of Education, University of Ulster, Londonderry, UK; [b]Department of Education, Queen's University Belfast, Belfast, UK

> In post-conflict and divided societies, global citizenship education has been described as a central element of peacebuilding education, whereby critical pedagogy is seen as a tool to advance students' thinking, transform their views and promote democratic behaviours. The present study investigates understandings of and attitudes to global citizenship and the challenges faced in its implementation. Teacher interviews highlight lack of time and resources for critical reflection and dialogue. Where opportunities for relevant training are provided, this can benefit critical engagement. Boundaries of educational systems and structures also influence pupils' understandings of the issues as evidenced in questionnaire findings. We argue that critical pedagogies may be limited unless criticality and activism transcend local and global issues and are applied to schools themselves. Emotional engagement may be required for teachers to claim the space to critically reflect and share with colleagues within and beyond their sectors in order to enable critical discourse amongst pupils.

Introduction

Education for peacebuilding, which goes beyond the cessation of violence and conflict and addresses structural and cultural violence, emphasises the concepts of local and global peace. While Fraser (2005) relates peacebuilding to specific concepts such as economic redistribution, cultural recognition and political representation, Reardon (1988) argues that 'comprehensive peace education, then, also means global education' (xii) and Reardon and Snauwaert (2011) promote education for 'responsible global citizenship' (2). Global citizenship education could then be defined as education that aims to enable students to challenge power imbalances, to negotiate identities and, ultimately, to achieve greater equality, justice, democracy and peace via individual and societal transformation (Nussbaum 1997). As such, it entails transformative social and political learning, which Reardon (2009) argues is best achieved by Freirean dialogic methods of education, informed by a philosophical understanding of education as humanisation.

While dialogic pedagogies may have a major influence on approaches to peacebuilding and global citizenship education in practice, empirical research focusing on teachers' and pupils' understandings has been scarce, especially in relation to post-conflict societies (Quaynor 2012). Additionally, questions have been raised in relation to potential limitations of such educational initiatives where they are being implemented in segregated settings. This paper therefore aimed to address this gap in the literature in the context of Northern Ireland as a divided society emerging from past conflict and maintaining a segregated education system.

Shapiro (2002) highlights the potential of humanising education to promote equal and fair societies, especially post-conflict, and to enable individuals to appreciate diversity and their common humanity. Advocates of global citizenship thus place importance on humanisation and its potential for a unifying identity (Appiah 2006). Nussbaum (1996) suggests that global citizenship education, which emphasises responsibility to humankind and shared values, may be the foundation to transcend inequalities and injustice at global, national and local levels and, thus, to build and maintain sustainable peace. The potential for global citizenship education to contribute to the development of long-term peace and to overcome community divisions is particularly important in post-conflict societies (Davies 2005), where 'the concept of [national] citizenship must be regarded as problematic and contested from the outset' (Smith 2003, 24). In such societies, local identities are often used to reinforce community boundaries, supported by divergent collective memories (Conway 2003). As such, peacebuilding initiatives may be seen as attempts to dilute and de-value community identities. Delanty (2006) proposes that critical cosmopolitanism should be based on 'internal cognitive transformation' and does not require a global identity but rather should be rooted in social, cultural and national identities. However, an emphasis on these identities in post-conflict societies may be detrimental to the potential for global citizenship to bridge community divisions, and therefore balancing local and global identities through critical pedagogical discourse seems crucial in such contexts. Indeed, it has been suggested to focus on deconstructing identities (Bekerman and Zembylas 2012) by means of critical reflection on one's own culture and perspective taking of the 'other' (Turner 2002), whereby global citizenship could facilitate the formation of an overarching humanising identity that bridges community divisions. While some have criticised the very concept of global citizenship as utopian and impractical (Heater 2004) or questioned its universal inclusiveness (Marshall 2009), others have considered the challenges in implementing global citizenship education in ways that may effectively enable individual and societal transformation, in line with Freirean propositions of critical pedagogy.

Freire (1996) argues for a three-pronged approach to critical pedagogy aimed at societal transformation, involving critical reflection, dialogue and action. Dialogue and subsequent action are rooted in critical thinking, which involves a sense of common humanity, understanding of reality as ever-changing and moral courage to challenge inequalities and oppression. Critical reflection thus delves beneath surface meanings, to try to uncover root causes of oppression and ways to confront it, in turn leading to humanisation. In educational contexts, Giroux (1983) explains that critical pedagogy includes not only critical thinking, but also active participation, engagement with identities through the development of individuals' autobiographies, consideration of common human values, learning about inequalities and oppression and developing the skills to challenge these. Giroux (1983) argues that critical pedagogy needs to be underpinned by an emotional engagement and optimism in order for it to be transformative. Emotional engagement has been similarly highlighted in global citizenship education by Davies (2006), who claimed that 'outrage' was required to motivate change.

Critical pedagogy within global citizenship education poses its own challenges, especially regarding the concept of local and global interdependence, its disputed root causes and how these can be addressed (Andreotti 2006; Roman 2003). For teachers in post-conflict societies, additional difficulties arise, whether they focus on the local level, where divergent identities need to be negotiated, or on the global level, where divergent North/South agendas and Western values need to be analysed (Bickmore 2007).

Despite the move away from a banking approach to education, where pupils are regarded as passive recipients of knowledge (Freire 1970), to more student-centred and participatory pedagogies, tensions remain between reproductive and transformative agendas of global citizenship education (Johnson and Morris 2010). Within post-conflict societies, concerns have been raised about the potential reproduction of societal divisions through the education system, official and hidden curricula (Gallagher 2005a), whereby local and global citizenship education has been under particular scrutiny (Smith 2010).

Based on theoretical and empirical research in the Netherlands, Veugelers (2011a) suggested that global citizenship education is indeed implemented differently in differing educational contexts. Analysing teacher interview data about understandings and practices relating to global citizenship education, he identified three main categories of global citizenship education: open, moral and social-political. Open global citizenship was found to result from teachers' understanding that globalisation required pupils to acquire knowledge about other cultures and to be open to new experiences. Moral global citizenship centred around appreciation of difference and diversity, increasing opportunities and taking responsibility towards humanity, at both local and global levels. The third category, which resonates strongly with Freirean principles of societal transformation, involves critical understanding of social-political relationships and challenging inequalities. Most teachers in this study opted for moral global citizenship and appeared reluctant to engage with social-political issues. Veugelers acknowledges divergent interpretations of global citizenship and argues for a multiple perspective approach incorporating all three understandings in order for students to develop their own perspectives. Noting social and cultural segregation in the Dutch education system, Veugelers cautions that while links between school and community are clearly important, orientation to the plural society and widening horizons are necessary in order to avoid reinforcing community identities and to develop shared and humanising discourses across community boundaries.

Theoretical framework

In the light of the above, the theoretical framework for this research draws on literature relating to critical pedagogies in peacebuilding and global citizenship education. In particular, we aimed to explore how Freirean principles of critical reflection, dialogue and action are evidenced in teachers' and pupils' reported understandings of global citizenship education in the context of a post-conflict society. In addition, based on work by Nussbaum (1996, 1997) and others, issues of local and global identities were explored and self-reported attitudes towards diversity and global inter-dependence examined. Finally, we aimed to discover the extent to which global citizenship education in a post-conflict society maps onto Veugelers' (2011b) open, moral and social-political categories.

Given the paucity of empirical evidence on dialogic pedagogies and global citizenship in the context of peacebuilding education (Quaynor 2012), this paper, drawing on analysis of both teacher and pupil data, will contribute to contemporary debates on dialogic pedagogy, global citizenship and peacebuilding by exploring and comparing teachers' discourses and pupils' understandings of global citizenship in the context of a post-conflict society. Veugelers (2011b) suggests that educational segregation and the potential for subsequent differential implementation of global citizenship may impede a positive impact on pupils and, more broadly, on societal cohesion, even in the context of a relatively peaceful society such as the Netherlands. This paper thus aimed to explore how such concerns may be reflected in the context of a post-conflict and divided society. The research questions were:

- How do teacher and pupil understandings of and attitudes to global citizenship reflect Freirean concepts of critical reflection, dialogue and action?

- What roles do humanisation and emotional engagement play in teachers' conceptualisations of global citizenship education and to what extent is this reflected in pupils' understandings and attitudes?
- Do approaches to global citizenship education map onto Veugelers' categorisation and do they vary systematically by school sector? To what extent are potential variations reflected in pupils' understandings and attitudes?

Context

The research was conducted in Northern Ireland as a relevant case study to examine global citizenship education in the context of a post-conflict and divided society. After a long history of identity-based conflict (Muldoon et al. 2007) between Catholics/Nationalists/Republicans, of whom the majority wish for unification with the Republic of Ireland, and Protestants/Unionists/Loyalists, of whom the majority wish to remain part of the UK (Cairns and Darby 1998), Northern Ireland underwent a peace process that culminated in the 1998 Belfast/Good Friday Agreement.

Despite decreased political violence, social segregation persists (Nolan 2012). The education system remains divided at primary and post-primary levels – the majority of Protestant pupils attend 'Controlled' schools, whilst the majority of Catholic pupils attend 'Maintained' schools, with about 5% attending 'Integrated' schools (Department of Education 2011). In contrast to Controlled and Maintained schools, Integrated schools are integrated by religion, gender and achievement. A few schools at both levels teach in the Irish medium, with mostly Catholic pupils.

All main education sectors, although differing in terms of management structure and ethos, receive full government funding and employ the same curriculum (Smith 2001). Issues relating to peacebuilding and citizenship, including local and global interconnections, equality and social justice, and democracy and active participation, are particularly evident in Local and Global Citizenship education in post-primary schools as well as in Personal Development and Mutual Understanding and the World Around us in the Primary Curriculum, although they are intended to infuse all subject areas (CCEA 2007a, 2007b).

Research methods

The current paper is based on data collected as part of a project that monitored and evaluated the global dimension in Northern Ireland schools. We draw on qualitative data from teacher focus groups and interviews, supported by quantitative findings from a pupil questionnaire to facilitate data triangulation as proposed by mixed-methods researchers (Johnson and Onwuegbuzie 2004).

Nine focus groups with teachers (not necessarily specialised in teaching global issues) included 2 to 16 participants in each group. The purposive sample comprised primary ($n = 4$) and post-primary schools ($n = 5$) from the main education sectors (including Controlled, Maintained, Integrated and one Irish-medium school) and schools situated in both urban and rural areas. Follow-up focus groups were held in seven of these schools at the end of the school year to assess changes that might impact on views and practices.

Similarly, purposive sampling was employed to recruit participants to 17 semi-structured interviews with teachers responsible for the delivery of local and global citizenship, and 18 follow-up interviews were conducted (in one school, two teachers held the post and both participated at follow-up). Focus groups and interviews with teachers took 30–90 minutes.

Finally, a questionnaire survey was completed by 401 pupils from 22 schools across Northern Ireland, again representing all main education sectors (see Niens and Reilly 2010 for the full research report). This sample included 141 males (35%) and 260 females (65%).

The study was approved by the School of Education's Research Ethics Committee at Queen's University Belfast. Schools were initially approached in writing and, once the principal had agreed, informed consent was obtained from teachers as well as all parents and pupils in identified Year 5 and Year 9 classes (8–9 and 12–13 years old).

Questions for teacher focus groups and interviews explored training, support and resources as well as understandings of key elements of the global dimension including global citizenship, the challenges they faced in implementation and whether or not they saw these as particular given the context of past conflict.

Qualitative data were transcribed and analysed thematically – themes were initially developed independently by each of the two researchers and then synthesised in an iterative process of discussion, theoretical reflection, searching for counter-examples and re-writing, until consensus was reached. In the following section, we provide an in-depth account (Braun and Clarke 2006) of a theoretically derived set of sub-themes, namely understandings of, and attitudes to, global citizenship and the challenges faced in the implementation of it.

The pupil questionnaire[1] entailed demographic questions and items relevant to global citizenship (e.g. attitudes to diversity and the environment, current and intended behaviours and school learning) and took about 30 minutes to complete. Data were analysed using descriptive statistics and analyses of variance were applied to check for potential school type differences where appropriate (see Niens and Reilly 2010 for details).

Findings are reported under five headings:

(1) aims of global citizenship,
(2) understandings of interdependence: emotional engagement,

(3) attitudes to diversity: humanisation,
(4) school approaches and differences,
(5) implementing global citizenship: challenges and trends.

Results

Aims of global citizenship

The teachers we interviewed expressed much enthusiasm about teaching global issues. In line with previous research (Holden 2006), pupil survey results also clearly indicated enjoyment of and engagement with global issues, with 75% of pupils reporting that they enjoyed learning about it a bit or a lot and 80% stating that they sometimes or often thought about how people live in other parts of the world. Teachers' understandings of the aims of global citizenship education focused mainly on pupil engagement and awareness raising. Almost all teachers emphasised the 'very insular' nature of Northern Ireland and hoped that teaching about global issues could open pupils' attitudes to other people, cultures and countries:

> You are opening their eyes and opening their ears and opening all their senses to other cultures and if you can only give a fraction of that, because quite often it's not happening at home, it's not happening outside in their community ... (Teacher, Controlled grammar school)

While this could be characterised as pragmatism, arguably it might be described as indicative of a lack of ambition, unlikely to result in the sort of challenges to identities, intergroup attitudes and an analysis of divergent perspectives that are integral to peace education (Salomon 2004). Indeed, developing superordinate identities was not mentioned by any of the teachers. Nevertheless, most thought that learning about global issues would positively impact on pupils' attitudes to diversity in the local and global context, although there was a parallel notion that for some pupils, increased awareness could reaffirm stereotypical views and local identities:

> ... definitely less conservative in their ideas in most cases. At the same time, I think there is a very small element that this has heightened their conservatism or heightened their sectarian views ... (Teacher, Maintained grammar school)

Findings were ambiguous with regard to whether or not pupils' community identities were challenged. Over half (53%) of pupils identified most strongly as 'Northern Irish', while traditional identifications of Catholic and Protestant pupils with British or Irish identities were ranked first by only 25% of respondents. This accords with recent research that highlights growing popularity of the category 'Northern Irish', which has been described as a 'common, superordinate ingroup' uniting Catholics and

Protestants (Schmid et al. 2009, 464), although affiliation to this category does not necessarily alter support for a United Ireland or the Union with Great Britain (Trew 1998). However, local identities predominated, as only 4% of pupils identified most as 'European people', while 41% identified least with 'People of the world'. Global citizenship education has been proposed as a tool to provide a superordinate identity, which may bridge community divisions and ultimately contribute to peacebuilding in post-conflict societies (Davies 2005). While our findings clearly demonstrate teachers' and pupils' engagement and interest in global issues, they also suggest that the development of a global identity was not seen as a goal of global citizenship education and that local identities may remain unchallenged by teaching and learning. Considering the potential of global citizenship education to heal community divisions in South Africa, Staeheli and Hammett (2010) caution that, '… it is difficult to see how any of the different forms of cosmopolitanism can, on their own, counteract the experiences of violence and inequality that students and communities in divided societies have confronted' (24). This may be particularly questionable where critical discourse around different notions of local and global identities is absent and where the goal of global citizenship is limited to awareness raising.

Understandings of interdependence: affective engagement

Teachers' understandings of interdependence were often limited by a lack of articulation between the local and global dimensions, which was equally evident in pupil focus-group data reported elsewhere (Niens and Reilly 2012). However, all teachers interviewed reported that environmental issues were part of their curricular and extra-curricular activities and some used environmentalism as a lens to introduce the concept of global interdependence.

Clearly the perception that this was an uncontroversial way of introducing pupils to a global perspective, coupled with widely available NGO input into the classroom, made teaching about the environment appealing to some teachers. This also appeared to be the only topic where Freire's three elements of critical pedagogies, critical reflection, dialogue and action, were explicitly articulated and inter-linked by teachers:

> So you are always teaching them the facts first … and then getting them to think beyond that. What's fact or opinion – looking at who is for conserving Antarctica, who is going to exploit it? (Teacher, Controlled secondary school)

This emphasis on the environment was echoed in pupils' survey responses, where 45% of pupils reported that they had learnt a lot about it. In relation to pupils' attitudes to environmental activism, the vast majority either agreed or strongly agreed that recycling rubbish (94%) and saving water (79%) make a difference for the environment locally and globally.

In contrast to the relative ease with which interviewees incorporated interdependence into teaching about the environment, even at primary level, some teachers saw economic and geopolitical interdependence as an unsuitable topic for younger pupils, or largely irrelevant to older ones:

> I think that to an extent, especially the younger ones, it's somewhere else, it doesn't matter, it's not going to affect them. They very much live in a small world. (Teacher, Maintained grammar school)

As such, the dialogic discourse that permeated much of the widely discussed teaching about the environment was largely absent in the teacher data in relation to issues of trade, consumerism and debt, which usually only emerged when prompted. Even then, teachers often associated the global economy with the idea of pupils visiting other countries for holidays, future study or work opportunities, consistent with Roman's (2003) conception of consumption of cultural difference.

Challenging inequalities and oppression is central to dialogical approaches (Freire 1996; Giroux 1983), however, teachers' conceptualisations and the ways in which they addressed global power imbalances varied substantially. In many schools, global citizenship began with involvement in European exchange programmes and some interviews were clearly influenced by Eurocentric notions. While some teachers did not query this, a few expressed a desire to widen their scope:

> Em, I think that to some extent Europe has been a comfort zone because it's relatively close and it's relatively similar and so on. Em, and what I would like us to do, em, is maybe to start and think about taking part in … a [global] North/South project. (Teacher, Controlled primary school)

Where global citizenship education was connected to the global South, it was almost always associated with fundraising, poverty and the desire to help and support those in need:

> That fund raising would go in the direction of an African school. … And I always thought it would be nice to have that sort of strong link with another school somewhere in Africa that we could support in some sort of way. (Teacher, Controlled primary school)

As Andreotti (2006) argues, such conceptualisations highlight the potential for stereotypical thinking and perpetuation of Eurocentric assumptions, again reflected in the pupil survey findings, which indicated some naivety and an element of blame in relation to causes of global poverty. Bad governance was regarded as the most or second most important cause of poverty by 60% of pupils, followed by war (40%), debts (35%), history of deprivation (27%) and colonial occupation (24%). In relation to potential solutions to poverty, 69% of respondents indicated that stopping wars and conflicts was the best or second best way to help poor countries, followed by 57% who rated increased trade of goods as the best or second best way and 51% who considered that giving poor countries money or cancelling debts was the best or second best way to help them.

Some teachers interviewed emphasised the importance of learning about and accepting one's responsibilities in a global context and this was related to political participation, consumerism and the environment. In line with Giroux's (1983) and Davies' (2006) calls for emotional engagement, one teacher saw such notions rooted in critical reflection and the search for underlying meanings, as well as a strong emotional reaction to inequality, which could precipitate activism and generalise to other areas:

> You would hope that it would be built on as they get older and tackle the more difficult issues. That they would understand the underlying reasons for, e.g. poverty in certain countries and that it's not just because the country is mismanaged, there is a lot more to do with it, and that would leave some sense of outrage in some, and a desire to be involved. (Teacher, Maintained primary school)

This quote clearly reflects the proposition that critical discourse and democratic engagement through education encourage students to challenge social inequalities and ultimately to transform society (Freire and Macedo 1995). However, this was a rather isolated testament to the potential impact of global citizenship learning. In addition, the pupil survey suggested that while respondents valued activism for change relating to the environment, economy and poverty, and were prepared to make lifestyle changes as a positive contribution to these issues, there was little evidence of strong emotional engagement or outrage. In relation to the economy, about two thirds of the sample (68%) agreed or strongly agreed that buying Fair Trade chocolate helps to improve someone's life, while 84% agreed or strongly agreed that donating money for a country in crisis makes a difference for the people there. There was much less enthusiasm for taking part in demonstrations against child labour, with 60% agreeing that it wouldn't change anything anyway and another 16% being uncertain. Pupils' responses appeared to reflect their assessment of the effectiveness of economic and alternative responses to global poverty, with lifestyle changes seen as essential, charity donations as most effective and demonstrations as least effective.

It was also noteworthy that when teachers referred to activism it was usually related to extra-curricular activities (e.g. eco-clubs, environmental awareness groups and NGO-supported groups). While this highlights the central role of schools in developing activism beyond, as well as through, the curriculum, research by McMurray and Niens (2012) indicates that in post-conflict societies with segregated education systems, vested community allegiances with specific NGOs and political agendas may limit the potential for citizenship education to bridge community divisions.

Attitudes to diversity: humanisation

By far the most prevalent issue that teachers included in their conceptualisations of global citizenship was respect for other cultures. This mainly referred to other countries or to immigrants in Northern Ireland, but only in a few cases was it associated with local Catholic/Protestant relations. Breaking down racial stereotypes was seen as a core issue of global citizenship and while a lack of ethnic diversity in the classroom was specifically lamented in rural schools, it was admitted that some local communities might not be tolerant towards incomers:

> ... we had no immigrant children and there aren't as far as I know any immigrant families living within the village. There were some individuals who were 'encouraged' to leave the community ... (Teacher, Controlled primary school)

Wider community influences thus appeared to affect interviewees' perceptions of what was possible and sensible to teach in the classroom. Although few teachers reported that they had experienced negative responses from parents, many more worried about potentially challenging locally prevalent attitudes. When asked about the main challenge of teaching in this area, a teacher from a rural Controlled Primary school in a very traditional area stated:

> Obviously you're not wanting to say, you know, to say, 'Well your daddy or mummy's wrong'.

These community influences as well as the more immediate classroom context appeared to contribute to a lack of confidence in teaching respect for other communities for some teachers, who found the controversial elements of this emotionally challenging, an acknowledged issue in dialogic approaches (Galtung 1996). One teacher in a school within a deprived urban area stated:

> ... their [pupils'] views are often very different to my views and they do have views that they bring from home and the outside world that, in terms of whether, you know ... beliefs that they hold about different countries and nationalities that ethically sit very sharply with me. I find it very uncomfortable. (Teacher, Controlled secondary school)

Teachers therefore acknowledged the difficulties of addressing attitudes to diversity, and again the pupil data reflect this. A large majority of pupils said any European (73%) and any African (72%) should be allowed to come to Northern Ireland if there are jobs, and attitudes to immigrants moving into Northern Ireland were generally positive (40% supported free entry to the country). However, a sizeable minority of about a quarter of respondents demonstrated less liberal attitudes to both groups.

Some interviewees highlighted the need for sensitivity when dealing with the Northern Ireland conflict, which in some communities remains an emotive issue (Cummings et al. 2009). Children, who have not directly experienced the conflict and who may have little knowledge of historical facts, nevertheless may retain a strong community identity and concomitant feelings about historical and current events. One teacher from a rural school situated in an area relatively untouched by the conflict explained that they did not tackle community relations because they felt that their pupils held no prejudice and talking about it might introduce sectarian ideas:

> ... when we started doing a few things, it was nearly like we were putting ideas into their head ... so, we kinda did to a certain extent step back a little bit from that ... (Teacher, Maintained primary school)

Concerns about introducing stereotypes and prejudiced thinking through classroom discussion particularly for young children have long been highlighted in the literature (Aboud and Doyle 1996). However, there is some evidence that critically engaged discussion about racism in early childhood classrooms actually moderates children's attitudes (Katz 2003).

While avoidance of sensitive issues featured strongly in the interviews, echoing previous research in Northern Ireland (McCully 2006), some interviewees reported that changing demographics, the new curriculum and active teaching methods are more conducive to addressing global issues and diversity than was formerly the case:

> ... but now as society moves forward, it's much more positive than it would have been. I think pupils now feel they have the space to express their opinion and be accepted so I think that is a positive thing. (Teacher, Controlled grammar school)

Linkages between sectarianism and racism were sometimes explicit but more frequently remained implicit, with pupils expected to extend and connect learning about treating migrants fairly to Catholic/Protestant relationships in Northern Ireland. A few teachers explicitly used conflicts in other countries to address local divisions:

> ... as a teacher of Spanish I would, you know, discuss very explicitly with the pupils the difference between the Spanish culture and the separatist Basque area and their struggle for independence. So, we would compare that to the Northern Irish versus UK, Irish conflict. (Teacher Maintained grammar school)

Such connections between local and global conflict using critical reflection and discourse were rare but highlighted how global citizenship could use Freirean principles to bridge community divisions. Exploring representations of conflict in Canadian curricula and finding few explicit connections between local and global conflict in these policy documents, Bickmore (2006) emphasises that, 'To contribute to citizenship education for democratic agency, explicit curriculum can and must delve into the unsafe but real world of social and political conflicts and injustices that defy simple negotiated settlement ...' (37). Our findings indicate that in the context of peacebuilding in post-conflict societies, global citizenship education practice cannot be disentangled from the complex nexus of tacit understandings of the rules, norms and tensions that characterise existing local intra- and inter-community relationships. However, critical pedagogies may be crucial to enable explicit negotiation of such issues through dialogue and reflection, which may enable action and ultimately, societal transformation for peacebuilding.

School approaches and differences

Although we cannot generalise from either sample, the data suggested that while teachers in all sectors reported similar aims, approaches appeared to differ by school sector in ways consistent with school ethos and traditions and which broadly appeared consistent with Veugelers' (2011a) categorisation of global citizenship education.

Reflecting an 'open global citizenship' approach (Veugelers 2011b), which emphasises learning about other countries and openness to new experiences, teachers in Controlled Protestant schools often focused on the development of international links and projects but rarely mentioned an ethos driving the whole sector to incorporate a community relations or charitable focus. In Controlled Post-Primary schools, these international links appeared to be explicitly oriented towards employability:

> ... if they [pupils] want to do a degree or such like that their direct competitors are people in India ... I try regularly to let them know that they are possibly not looking for jobs in NI but for jobs somewhere in the world in the future because that's what is going to have to happen. (Teacher, Controlled grammar school)

Extension of employability concerns to other countries might present opportunities to challenge stereotypes of the Global South as poverty-stricken and to develop more differentiated understandings of global power relationships. While pupils attending Controlled schools were less likely than those from other sectors to rate learning about African countries, other European countries, and diversity as important (Table 1), the survey did not focus extensively on pupils' economic understandings and attitudes to international employability and this may be an area for future research.

Moral global citizenship centres around appreciating diversity, increasing opportunities and taking responsibility towards humanity (Veugelers 2011a). This appeared consistent with approaches in the Maintained Catholic sector, where the prevailing ethos included historical associations with international missionary work and charitable traditions (Montgomery and Smith 1997). A teacher from a Maintained primary school explained:

> I suppose it's part of your religion program to do that [global issues] throughout Lent, to make children aware that there are people suffering out there, so it comes from the religious aspect first in respect of Christianity. Then as a Christian you have a duty to look after these other people and yes it is done on a global dimension.

Global responsibility thus featured highly in teacher understandings in the Catholic Maintained sector. The pupil survey data also indicated that pupils attending Maintained schools were significantly more likely than those attending Controlled schools to welcome migrants to Northern Ireland and to view the international community, the government and every individual as responsible for solving conflict and supporting peace. They also consistently reported learning more about global issues in school than pupils in other sectors (Table 1). While Veugelers noted that a moral approach applied not only at global but also at local level, a focus on local community divisions in relation to the past conflict was less evident in the Catholic Maintained school findings emerging from our data.

This dimension was, however, emphasised in the Integrated school sector, where the global dimension was seen as inherent in an existing ethos of promoting diversity and respect (McGlynn 2011), first and foremost regarding Catholic and Protestant relations, but extending to other minority cultures within Northern Ireland. One teacher from an Integrated post-primary school explained:

> … by the very nature of being Integrated, we acknowledge differences, we accept differences and we celebrate sameness as well as diversity …

Challenging prejudice was thus one of the focal points for teachers interviewed in Integrated schools. Pupil survey data revealed that pupils in Integrated schools were significantly more likely than others to believe that it was important to learn about conflict resolution in school (Table 1). Similar to Veugelers' (2011a) research in the Netherlands, there was little consistent evidence of social-political global citizenship, which may mirror most closely Freirean notions of critical pedagogies for social transformation, though a few teachers indicated some recognition of such an approach. In a divided educational system, it may be expected that different sectors approach global citizenship in ways that are consistent with existing practices. While different approaches might potentially exacerbate community divisions, these differences in expertise clearly present opportunities for collaborative work between the sectors, allowing teachers to learn from each other. Gallagher (2005b) highlights that learning within separate school

Table 1. Analysis of variance to test for denominational school type differences.

Question	Item	Group (n)	Mean	SD	Df	F
How important is it to learn about the following?	How people live in other European countries (e.g. their history, traditions, music, food)	Controlled (144)	5.50	2.47	2	6.48***
		Maintained (168)	6.46	2.49		
		Integrated (57)	6.39	2.38		
Response format from 1 (not important at all) to 10 (extremely important)	How people live in other continents such as Africa or Asia (e.g. their history, traditions, music, food)	Controlled (143)	5.51	2.57	2	4.99***
		Maintained (166)	6.21	2.39		
		Integrated (56)	6.61	2.60		
	Differences and similarities between people and groups	Controlled (141)	6.01	2.70	2	4.88***
		Maintained (168)	6.81	2.50		
		Integrated (55)	7.07	2.77		
	Conflict resolution	Controlled (143)	6.14	2.80	2	4.26*
		Maintained (158)	6.86	2.90		
		Integrated (53)	7.34	2.80		
If there is conflict between groups or nations …	It is the responsibility of the international community to solve them	Controlled (192)	2.49	.70	2	3.58*
		Maintained (112)	2.21	.81		
		Integrated (30)	2.37	.72		
Response format from 1 (agree strongly) to 4 (disagree strongly)	It is the responsibility of our government to solve them	Controlled (105)	2.26	.83	2	6.69***
		Maintained (120)	2.64	.81		
		Integrated (30)	2.62	.85		
	It is everybody's responsibility to support peace (e.g. through economic boycotts, demonstrations)	Controlled (103)	1.98	.73	2	5.31**
		Maintained (121)	1.64	.77		
		Integrated (30)	1.77	.90		
How do you feel about people	European countries	Controlled (155)	2.76	.93	2	11.70***

(*Continued*)

Table 1. (Continued).

Question	Item	Group (n)	Mean	SD	Df	F
from other countries coming to live in Northern Ireland?		Maintained (81)	3.25	.89		
		Integrated (61)	3.02	1.04		
Response format from 1 (anybody from there should be allowed to come here for work) to 4 (nobody from there should be allowed to come here for work)	African countries	Controlled (156)	2.80	1.01	2	9.95***
		Maintained (181)	3.27	.89		
		Integrated (56)	3.02	.99		

Notes: Post-hoc analysis through Bonferoni, where equal variances could be assumed, or Dunnett C, where homogeneity of variance tests were significant; *significance level < .05; **significance level < .01; ***significance level < .001.

sectors begs the challenge of a lack of 'diversity in terms of experience and perspective' (166) and this clearly seems to refer not only to issues of local but also of global relevance. Gallagher warns that it would be simplistic to argue that separate schools are solely responsible for maintaining societal divisions, but the opportunities presented by cross-sector partnerships should not be neglected, given they provide a context where alternative perspectives can be explored and critical discourses developed using a dialogic approach. Such collaborations had already been experienced by some interviewees who highlighted their benefits:

> Em, we have stayed very good friends, but all that [school collaboration] has been beneficial for us … who are at different schools in the same town, it gave us opportunities to walk in and out of each other's schools, you know, and bring students across to each other's schools, so it helps break down some of those barriers. (Teacher, Integrated post-primary school)

School partnerships have proliferated in Northern Ireland in recent years and shared education has been firmly incorporated into public and policy discourses around education (Connolly, Purvis, and O'Grady 2013), whereby its potential to contribute to community relations has gained increasing public acknowledgement. Recognising the potential of sharing between sectors for peacebuilding is important not only directly with regards to reconciliation (Hughes et al. 2010), but also indirectly regarding the hidden curriculum, which otherwise may impact differentially on teaching and learning between sectors.

Implementing global citizenship: challenges and trends

Some schools took a structured approach to global issues in teaching and learning, but others relied on analysis and extension of their existing provision and activities in order to limit additional demands on teaching staff. One teacher explained:

> But I mean they are already covering [it], the work's already being done, so we just need them maybe to make the pupils more aware of where or how it is connecting globally. (Teacher, Maintained grammar school)

While this approach had the advantage of alleviating staff concerns, there was limited evidence of additional time being provided to develop a knowledge base, which might inform critical discourses in the classroom and thus contribute to a dialogic development of understandings around global citizenship. In fact, lack of time was one of the most frequently reported challenges, whether for identifying relevant resources and training opportunities, for critical reflection and/or dialogue with colleagues. Many teachers accepted that global issues were becoming embedded in resources but bemoaned the lack of available lesson plans that could minimise preparation on their part, calling into question their level of commitment to critical engagement with global issues.

Some interviewees expressed concerns that the current curriculum is overloaded and were sceptical about adding local and global citizenship as yet another subject or initiative for which they would be accountable, with a dearth of specific training and materials. Other teachers did not see this as an obstacle:

> But, specific training, no, nothing is available that I'm aware of. We just muddle through ourselves and, and try and progress and bring in as many ideas together. But we're confident, we don't feel under supported, we feel we are happy, I think there's a lot out there ... (Teacher, Controlled grammar school)

In the absence of training opportunities and given time pressures, such confidence may be misplaced. Teacher knowledge and experience are clearly invaluable. However, these alone seem an insecure basis for the development of critical discourses in classrooms. Freire (1987) suggests that teachers need more than subject knowledge and methodological expertise – they must develop a clear political understanding of the issues explored, which necessitates time for critical reflection and opportunities for discourses amongst teachers themselves.

In some schools, little changed over the year between interviews, while others reported specific changes, for example, one school had moved to a new building, others had experienced significant staff changes, or a rapid expansion in enrolment or had begun to offer new examinations. In another school, the retirement of a particularly supportive principal led to a marked reduction in global citizenship activities and teacher attitudes and discussions were notably more muted than in the previous year, underlining the importance of senior management support for such initiatives (Osler 2008).

At post-primary level, several schools had adopted a more strategic approach to global citizenship, which seemed largely curriculum-led. This was less evident at Primary level, where teachers expressed uncertainty about expectations for teaching global issues:

> Government wise, I think they kind of want us to do it, but there's very little direction, it's kind of put out there as, like, a big wish, we would like you to bring the global dimension in, but they're not specifically saying do this, do that ... (Teacher, Maintained urban primary school)

A few teachers discussed the need to politicise issues such as poverty and to take a more critical approach, and one noted development in their own understanding of global issues, illustrating the potential of critical pedagogies and training to promote learning and improve teaching practices:

> I would have done it [Africa] as a 'mud huts' aspect of it, which is wrong, you know, so I think for me personally, for me that's one area you know I've probably changed my own opinion and the way I would teach that to the children ... (Teacher, Controlled primary school)

Over the course of the year, there was little evidence of any systematic development of organisational or pedagogical approaches, rather the picture was one of isolated change in response to situational factors. Coupled with the structural limitations on practice such as limited time, limited teacher knowledge and experience and, perhaps equally importantly, the contextual limitations of a divided and post-conflict society, there was little evidence for development of critical dialogic pedagogies, nor of emotional engagement that might challenge the status quo.

Conclusion

In the context of a post-conflict society, this paper explored how Freirean principles of critical reflection, dialogue and action are evidenced in teachers' and pupils' understandings of global citizenship education, the roles identities, humanisation and emotional engagement play in this and how different school sectors may approach it. In the following, we revisit the research questions to discuss the findings in the light of the theoretical framework.

How do teacher and pupil understandings of and attitudes to global citizenship reflect Freirean concepts of critical reflection, dialogue and action?

Despite teachers' and pupils' enthusiasm for teaching and learning about global issues, which echoed previous research evidence (Edge, Khamsi, and Bourn 2008), Freirean concepts of critical reflection, dialogue and action were only rarely evident in teacher interviews and reflected in pupils' questionnaire responses. Lack of time for teaching, researching and reflection was seen as a major impediment to implementing global citizenship education effectively. This, coupled with a lack of relevant training, appeared to result in many teachers adopting an instrumental approach, which Winter (2007), referring to Education for Sustainable Development, noted did not enable critical reflection.

While environmental issues had universal appeal, demonstrated by sound understandings of inter-relationships between local action and global impact, which were expressed in pupils' sense of efficacy, such understandings were not reliably translated into other areas of global citizenship. As such, the potential role of environmental learning as an entry point should be considered, not only for understanding interdependence, but also for developing skills of critical engagement, discourse and activism, which could be applied to less well-developed areas such as trade, consumerism and debt. Dunlap and Van Liere (2008) argue that while the environmental paradigm has become widely accepted, critical analysis of wider issues of economic growth and impact is needed to effectively challenge the status quo.

What roles do humanisation and emotional engagement play in teachers' conceptualisations of global citizenship education and to what extent is this reflected in pupils' attitudes and understandings?

Avoidance of engagement with issues relating to inequalities and power imbalances was particularly evident with regards to understandings of the concept of interdependence as well as conflict and continuing divisions in Northern Ireland. Humanisation was evident in some teachers' pedagogical approaches to global citizenship, while emotional engagement emerged in other teachers' approaches, but only rarely did the two co-exist. There also appeared to be a dichotomy between teachers who regarded addressing diversity and conflict as essential, and those preferring to concentrate on common humanity. While the latter approach has been considered inadequate to challenge global inequalities by theorists such as Parekh (2003) and Andreotti (2006), the former may fail to address the development of a superordinate identity that has been considered essential to global citizenship and peacebuilding education (Nussbaum 1996). In fact, neither teachers' nor pupils' understandings of global citizenship indicated reconsideration of locally divided identities or the development of superordinate identities, which could bridge local and global community divisions. Global citizenship education for peacebuilding needs to go beyond advocacy of tolerance and common humanity to include critical reflection about the socially constructed meanings of identities and communities and their implications for societies (Bekerman 2009). According to Freire (1996) and Giroux (1983), critical pedagogy requires critical reflection, critical dialogue and action, underpinned by humanisation and emotional engagement, to achieve societal transformation. Thus, global citizenship should combine critical reflection and discourse on local identities and common humanity in order to promote peacebuilding at local and global levels.

Do approaches to global citizenship education map onto Veugelers' categorisation and do they vary systematically by school sector? To what extent are potential variations reflected in pupils' attitudes and understandings?

In the context of education for peacebuilding, we argue that a lack of critical engagement with issues of identity and conflict may be compounded by different approaches to global citizenship education in the various school sectors. While the sample included all main school types in Northern Ireland, it was not representative. However, teacher and pupil findings suggested divergence between school sectors, with different emphases on local community relations, charitable work and employability. Our findings are broadly consistent with the three approaches to global citizenship education identified by Veugelers (2011a), namely open, moral (including a local element) and socio-political. However, our data suggest that in Northern Ireland as a post-conflict society, the local element of the moral approach described by Veugelers (2011b) assumes a high level of importance. We therefore argue that a fourth category may be needed to describe an approach to global citizenship in post-conflict societies, which is inclusive of local identities and divisions.

Despite the widespread abandonment of what Freire (1970) termed a banking system of education, it has been noted that tensions between reproductive and transformative agendas of citizenship education remain (Johnson and Morris 2010). Societal divisions may be both reflected in and reproduced by educational structures and policies, and the boundaries and limitations these impose appear to translate into teachers' and pupils' understandings of global citizenship. We argue that this demonstrates how critical pedagogies can be restricted by structural and social boundaries as well as by more mundane time and resource concerns. As such our research indicates that it may be necessary for teachers to transcend these boundaries in the first place, to engage in critical discourse beyond their own bounded school and local communities and to engage in cross-sector collaborations in order to facilitate critical reflection and discourse amongst their pupils, which may eventually transform society. The recent incorporation of shared education in Northern Irish policy (Connolly, Purvis, and O'Grady 2013) should provide opportunities for teachers to engage in such collaboration.

Shultz (2009, 10) stresses the need for global citizenship education to address both conflict and complexity. While acknowledging the long tradition of educators committed to social justice and peace education she nevertheless cautions that:

> History has demonstrated that educators become the foot soldiers of oppressive policy and regimes when they become compliant and disengaged (or perhaps distracted) through excessive accountability agendas, top-down reform discourses, and efficiency demands ... resulting in schools becoming places where society is learned rather than created.

Based on the findings in our research, we believe that changes within the education system to allow spaces for critical reflection, training and cross-school collaborations will not in themselves guarantee critical discourses relating to local and global issues taking place in the classroom and societal divisions being transformed. There is, in the first instance, a need for teachers to develop some sense of emotional engagement, to recognise and challenge existing structural and contextual limitations, in order to provide an opening to transformative learning amongst teachers and students and thereby to contribute to peacebuilding in society.

Funding

This research was funded by DfID through the Global Dimension in Schools (NI).

Note

1. Designed in conjunction with staff from the Centre for Global Education and the Global Dimension in Schools (NI) project.

References

Aboud, F., and A. B. Doyle. 1996. "Does Talk of Race Foster Prejudice or Tolerance in Children?" *Canadian Journal of Behavioural Science* 28 (3): 161–170.
Andreotti, V. 2006. "Soft Versus Critical Global Citizenship Education." *Development Education: Policy and Practice* 3 (4): 83–98.
Appiah, K. A. 2006. *Cosmopolitanism: Ethnics in a World of Strangers*. New York: Norton.
Bekerman, Z. 2009. "Identity versus Peace: Identity Wins." *Harvard Educational Review* 79 (1): 74–83.
Bekerman, Z., and M. Zembylas. 2012. *Teaching Contested Narratives. Identity, Memory and Reconciliation in Peace Education and beyond*. Cambridge: Cambridge University Press.

Bickmore, K. 2006. "Democratic Social Cohesion (Assimilation)? Representations of Social Conflict in Canadian Public School Curriculum." *Canadian Journal of Education* 29 (2): 13–40.

Bickmore, K. 2007. "Linking Global with Local: Cross-Cultural Conflict Education." In *Education, Conflict and Reconciliation: International Perspectives*, edited by F. Leach and M. Dunne, 237–252. Berne: Peter Lang.

Braun, V., and V. Clarke. 2006. "Using Thematic Analysis in Psychology." *Qualitative Research in Psychology* 3 (2): 77–101.

Cairns, E., and J. Darby. 1998. "The Conflict in Northern Ireland: Causes, Consequences, and Controls." *American Psychologist* 53 (7): 754–760.

Connolly, P., D. Purvis, and P. J. O'Grady. 2013. "Advancing Shared Education: A Report of the Ministerial Advisory Group." Accessed May 30, 2013. http://www.qub.ac.uk/schools/SchoolofEducation/MinisterialAdvisoryGroup/Filestore/Filetoupload,382123,en.pdf

Conway, B. 2003. "Active Remembering, Selective Forgetting, and Collective Identity: The Case of Bloody Sunday." *Identity: An International Journal of Theory and Research* 3 (4): 305–323.

Council for Curriculum, Examinations and Assessment (CCEA). 2007a. *The Northern Ireland Curriculum: Primary*. Belfast: CCEA.

Council for Curriculum, Examinations and Assessment (CCEA). 2007b. *The Statutory Curriculum at Key Stage 3: Rationale and Detail*. Belfast: CCEA.

Cummings, E. M., M. C. Goeke-Morey, A. C. Schermerhorn, C. E. Merrilees, and E. Cairns. 2009. "Children and Political Violence from a Social Ecological Perspective: Implications from Research on Children and Families in Northern Ireland." *Clinical Child and Family Psychology Review* 12 (1): 16–38.

Davies, L. 2005. "Teaching about Conflict through Citizenship Education." *International Journal of Citizenship and Teacher Education* 1 (2): 17–34.

Davies, L. 2006. "Global Citizenship: Abstraction or Framework for Action?" *Educational Review* 58 (1): 5–25.

Delanty, G. 2006. "The Cosmopolitan Imagination: Critical Cosmopolitanism and Social Theory." *British Journal of Sociology* 57 (1): 25–47.

Department of Education Northern Ireland. 2011. "Integrated Schools." Accessed September 17, 2013. http://www.deni.gov.uk/index/85-schools/10-types_of_-school-ni schools_pg/16-schoolsintegratedschools_pg.htm

Dunlap, R. E., and K. D. Van Liere. 2008. "The 'New Environmental Paradigm'." *The Journal of Environmental Education* 40 (1): 19–28.

Edge, K., K. Khamsi, and D. Bourn. 2008. *Exploring the Global Dimension in Secondary Schools*. London: IOE.

Fraser, N. 2005. "Reframing Justice In A Globalized World." *New Left Review* 36: 79–88.

Freire, P. 1970. *Pedagogy of the Oppressed*. New York: Continuum.

Freire, P. 1987. *Literacy: Reading the Word and the World*. London: Routledge.

Freire, P. 1996. *Pedagogy of the Oppressed*. London: Penguin Books.

Freire, P., and D. P. Macedo. 1995. "A Dialogue: Culture, Language and Race." *Harvard Educational Review* 65 (3): 377–403.

Gallagher, T. 2005a. "Balancing Difference and the Common Good: Lessons from a Post-Conflict Society." *Compare* 35 (4): 429–442.

Gallagher, T. 2005b. "Faith Schools and Northern Ireland: A Review of Research." In *Faith Schools: Consensus or Conflict?* edited by R. Gardner, J. Cairns, and D. Lawton, 156–165. London: Routledge Falmer.

Galtung, J. 1996. *Peace by Peaceful Means: Peace and Conflict, Development, & Civilization*. London: Sage and International Peace Research Association.

Giroux, H. 1983. *Theory and Resistance in Education: A Pedagogy for the Opposition*. London: Heinemann Educational.

Heater, D. 2004. *World Citizenship: Cosmopolitan Thinking and Its Opponents*. London: Continuum.

Holden, C. 2006. "Concerned Citizens: Children and the Future." *Education, Citizenship and Social Justice* 1 (3): 231–247.

Hughes, J., C. Donnelly, M. Hewstone, T. Gallagher, and K. Carlisle. 2010. *School Partnerships and Reconciliation: An Evaluation of School Collaboration in Northern Ireland*. Belfast: Queen's University Belfast.

Johnson, L., and P. Morris. 2010. "Towards a Framework for Critical Citizenship Education." *The Curriculum Journal* 21 (1): 77–96.

Johnson, R. B., and R. J. Onwuegbuzie. 2004. "Mixed Methods Research: A Research Paradigm Whose Time Has Come." *Educational Researcher* 33 (7): 14–26.

Katz, P. A. 2003. "Racists or Tolerant Multiculturalists? How Do They Begin?" *American Psychologist* 58 (11): 897–909.

Marshall, H. 2009. "Educating the European Citizen in the Global Age: Engaging with the Postnational and Identifying a Research Agenda." *Journal of Curriculum Studies* 41 (2): 247–267.

McCully, A. 2006. "Practitioner Perceptions of Their Role in Facilitating the Handling of Controversial Issues in Contested Societies: A Northern Irish Experience." *Educational Review* 58 (1): 51–65.

McGlynn, C. 2011. "Negotiating Difference in Post-Conflict Northern Ireland: An Analysis of Approaches to Integrated Education." *Multicultural Perspectives* 13 (1): 16–22.

McMurray, A., and U. Niens. 2012. "Citizenship and Social Capital in Northern Ireland." *Education, Citizenship and Social Justice* 7 (2): 207–221.

Montgomery, A., and A. Smith. 1997. *Values in Education in Northern Ireland*. Coleraine: University of Ulster, School of Education.

Muldoon, O. T., K. Trew, J. Todd, N. Rougier, and K. McLaughlin. 2007. "Religious and National Identity after the Belfast Good Friday Agreement." *Political Psychology* 28 (1): 89–103.

Niens, U., and J. Reilly. 2010. *Global Dimension in the Northern Ireland Curriculum: School Approaches, Teaching and Learning*. Belfast: Queen's University, Belfast, and University of Ulster.

Niens, U., and J. Reilly. 2012. "Education for Global Citizenship in a Divided Society? Young People's Views and Experiences." *Comparative Education* 48 (1): 103–118.

Nolan, P. 2012. *Northern Ireland Peace Monitoring Report Number One*. Belfast: Community Relations Council.

Nussbaum, M. C. 1996. "Patriotism and Cosmopolitanism." *Boston Review* 19 (5): 3–34.

Nussbaum, M. C. 1997. "Kant and Cosmopolitanism." In *Perpetual Peace: Essays on Kant's Cosmopolitan Ideal*, edited by J. Bohman and M. Lutz-Bachmann, 25–58. Cambridge, MA: MIT Press.

Osler, A. 2008. "Citizenship Education and the Ajegbo Report: Re-Imagining a Cosmopolitan Nation." *London Review of Education* 6 (1): 11–25.

Parekh, B. 2003. "Cosmopolitanism and Global Citizenship." *Review of International Studies* 29 (1): 3–17.

Quaynor, L. J. 2012. "Citizenship Education in Post-Conflict Contexts: A Review of the Literature." *Education, Citizenship and Social Justice* 7 (1): 33–57.

Reardon, B. 1988. *Comprehensive Peace Education: Educating for Global Responsibility*. New York: Teachers College Press.

Reardon, B. A. 2009. "Human Rights Learning: Pedagogies and Politics of Peace." Paper presented at the annual "Leccion Magistral", University of Puerto Rico, April 15.

Reardon, B. A., and D. T. Snauwaert. 2011. "Reflective Pedagogy, Cosmopolitanism, and Critical Peace Education for Political Efficacy: A Discussion of Betty A. Reardon's Assessment of the Field." *Factis Pax* 5 (1): 1–14.

Roman, L. G. 2003. "Education and the Contested Meanings of 'Global Citizenship'." *Journal of Educational Change* 4 (3): 269–293.

Salomon, G. 2004. "Does Peace Education Make a Difference in the Context of an Intractable Conflict?" *Peace and Conflict: Journal of Peace Psychology* 10 (3): 257–274.

Schmid, K., M. Hewstone, N. Tausch, E. Cairns, and J. Hughes. 2009. "Antecedents and Consequences of Social Identity Complexity: Intergroup Contact, Distinctiveness Threat, and Outgroup Attitudes." *Personality and Social Psychology Bulletin* 35 (8): 1085–1098.

Shapiro, S. 2002. "Pedagogy of Peace Education." In *Peace Education: The Concept, Principles, and Practices Around the World*, edited by G. Salomon and B. Nevo, 63–72. Mahwah, NJ: Lawrence Erlbaum Associates.

Shultz, L. 2009. "Conflict, Dialogue and Justice: Exploring Global Citizenship Education as a Generative Social Justice Project." *Journal of Contemporary Issues in Education* 4 (2): 3–13.

Smith, A. 2001. "Religious Segregation and the Emergence of Integrated Schools in Northern Ireland." *Oxford Review of Education* 27 (4): 559–575.

Smith, A. 2003. "Citizenship Education in Northern Ireland: Beyond National Identity?" *Cambridge Journal of Education* 33 (1): 15–32.

Smith, A. 2010. "The Influence of Education on Conflict and Peace Building." Paper commissioned for the EFA Global Monitoring Report 2011, "The Hidden Crisis: Armed Conflict and Education." Accessed October 17, 2013. http://unesco.atlasproject.eu/unesco/file/08577c2a-f356-4c63-93b1-a72cc7ce2e27/c8c7fe00-c770-11e1-9b21-0800200c9a66/191341e.pdf

Staeheli, L. A., and D. Hammett. 2010. "Educating the New National Citizen: Education, Political Subjectivity and Divided Societies." *Citizenship Studies* 14 (6): 667–680.

Trew, K. 1998. "The Northern Irish Identity." In *A Question of Identity*, edited by A. J. Kershen, 60–76. Aldershot: Ashgate.

Turner, B. S. 2002. "Cosmopolitan Virtue, Globalization and Patriotism." *Theory, Culture & Society* 19 (1–2): 45–63.

Veugelers, W. 2011a. "A Humanist Perspective on Moral Development and Citizenship Education." In *Education and Humanism*, edited by W. Veugelers, 9–34. Rotterdam: Sense.

Veugelers, W. 2011b. "The Moral and the Political in Global Citizenship: Appreciating Differences in Education." *Globalisation, Societies and Education* 9 (3–4): 473–485.

Winter, C. 2007. "Education for Sustainable Development and the Secondary Curriculum in English Schools: Rhetoric or Reality?" *Cambridge Journal of Education* 37 (3): 337–354.

Articulating injustice: an exploration of young people's experiences of participation in a conflict transformation programme that utilises the arts as a form of dialogue

Heather Knight

Institute of Education, Plymouth University, Plymouth, UK

> This paper reflects on a study that explores young people's engagement with the Art: a Resource for Reconciliation Over the World (ARROW) programme. The programme utilises the arts to promote critical dialogue amongst young people growing up in divided communities around the world. Dialogue has been criticised for its inability to tackle structural inequalities and for failing to include multiple voices and perspectives due to dominant languages and agendas. However, dialogue has also been heralded for its potential to promote democracy and resist narratives of discrimination that contribute to intercultural conflict. This paper focuses on the voices of young people involved in the Plymouth UK ARROW youth group. It proposes that arts approaches can complement verbal dialogue through their ability to transcend verbal language barriers, allow previously silenced narratives to be articulated and encourage people to think critically about themselves, humanity and the world.

Introduction

The need to address intercultural conflict and build more peaceful integrated communities has become a national concern in the UK. In the summer of 2011, rioting and looting erupted in a number of cities across England. A peaceful demonstration, following the fatal shooting of a man in London by the police, turned into violent clashes with police. This was said to be caused by unrest due to police discrimination against local Black[1] communities. The subsequent riots that spread across the country led to a number of debates about other possible causes. These ranged from discrimination, disadvantage and poverty, to opportunism, to government public funding cuts for youth provision, to bad parenting and Prime Minister David Cameron's notion of a 'broken society'. Whilst the causes of the riots and possible resolution strategies are contested, creative solutions are called for to address present-day conflicts (Lederach 1997).

This paper reflects on a dialogic approach proposed by international conflict mediator John Paul Lederach. Lederach (1997) professes the need to address the human element of conflict when conflicting communities live near to one another, bound up in hostile interactions, grievance, animosity, fear and stereotyping. This involves a, 'paradigmatic shift … in the movement away from concern with the resolution of issues towards a frame of reference that focuses on the restoration of relationships' (23–24). Rebuilding relationship involves the use of dialogue, providing opportunities for conflicting groups to see each other as 'humans-in-relationship' through expressing with one another aspects such as loss, anger and pain that are experienced as a result of conflict (26).

The approach has links with dialogic pedagogy, a form of political action that challenges unequal social structures through the practice of education. Popularised by international educator Paulo Freire (1996), dialogic pedagogy seeks to remove the 'banking' concept of domestication education whereby 'expert' educators 'fill' passive students with knowledge (57). This is replaced with liberation education that promotes critical dialogue amongst students focusing on their own 'preoccupations, doubts, hopes and fears' (77). It provides a 'process in which individuals analysing their own reality become aware of their prior, distorted perceptions and thereby come to have a new perception of that reality' (95). With greater awareness of social, cultural and political forces impacting on beliefs and experiences, comes the potential to make changes.

However, whilst dialogic pedagogy has been heralded for its potential to promote democracy (Freire 1996) and reconcile conflicting relationships (Lederach 1997), it is also criticised for its inability to tackle structural inequalities that maintain conflict between different social and cultural groups. Indeed, when working across diverse cultures, the voices and perspectives of more powerful groups are said to dominate (Spivak 1988). In addition, not everyone speaks the same language, yet dialogue has to take place on someone's terms and therefore issues exist in terms of who gets to speak and who sets the agenda (Burbules 2000).

This article compares verbal dialogue with arts-based dialogue, arguing that arts approaches can address some of the critiques. Based on Lederach and Freire's conceptualisations of dialogue for social transformation, it proposes that the arts can act as a form of dialogue, communicating through mediums such as painting, music, drama, dance and storytelling. It draws on data from a small-scale qualitative study with a global 'arts for conflict transformation' programme. The Art: a Resource for Reconciliation Over the World (ARROW) programme was founded in 2004 by David Oddie at the University College Plymouth St Mark and St John. Oddie initiated the programme as a social entrepreneurial response to events such as the UK northern 'race' riots, the events of 9/11 and increasing racial tensions in Britain. The ARROW programme was developed as a global programme in partnership with colleagues in the UK, South Africa, Palestine and Kosovo, later extending to additional countries.[2] Each partner organisation utilises the arts in a range of ways to address issues in their communities. Al Harah Theatre[3] in Beit Jala, Palestine uses theatre arts to bring 'compelling stories' to audiences throughout Palestine, the Arab world and beyond to emphasise 'human rights, democracy and freedom of expression as key components for a dynamic society' (www.alharah.org). The ARROW South Africa group in Durban[4] engage in drama, games, poetry, storytelling and art workshops as a means of local, national and international interpersonal exploration, with an emphasis on the role that interdependence plays in reconciliation and peace building.

In the summer of 2010, over 100 young people and their co-ordinators from around the world gathered for the ARROW Global Congress in Plymouth, UK. This event was described as 'a life transforming experience for participants' (www.theindracongress.com). Following this, the programme moved away from the university framework to become an independent global, social enterprise, working under the new name of the International Development of the Arts for Reconciliation (INDRA) Congress. The programme continues to grow and develop using a pattern of arts-based activities:

> This pattern involves young people and their co-ordinators in INDRA hubs undertaking conflict related projects in their own communities, and then sharing their experience both virtually and live with their peers across the world. (www.theindracongress.com)

A further global congress took place in Derry, Northern Ireland, during the first week in July 2013, as part of the INDRA congress. This paper does not extend to describe the diversity and richness of all events, nor does it purport to explore the complexity of the societies in which it operates. It reports on voices and experiences of young people involved in the initial ARROW programme, in Plymouth in the south west of England. It is likely that young people who took part in the global congresses would have moved on in their thinking and experiences. In this paper the quotes from young people represent the early stages of the work as the programme emerged. The paper discusses ways in which arts-based dialogue has encouraged young people to think critically about themselves, humanity and the world.

Contested approaches to diversity

I begin by examining contested approaches to diversity and dialogue. Different conceptualisations of diversity exist. Broadly speaking, these fall into 'celebrating diversity' or 'assimilating unity'. Contested views on diversity were debated in a special issue of *Compare* in 2007. Gallagher and Pritchard's (2007) article highlighted that pre-9/11, diversity debates argued between assimilation and multiculturalism. The latter, in the form of the multicultural model, began to win through. However, the authors posit that post-9/11, a shift back to the assimilation model occurred, through a national integration agenda. They questioned whether, 'elevation of similarity and commonality may be given precedence over the celebration of difference' (567).

The integration approach can be seen in the Community Cohesion strategy that was developed post-9/11. This approach followed the Cantle (2001) report that paved the way for Community Cohesion initiatives to address racial conflict on a community level. Cantle highlighted that poverty and lack of resources can lead to mutual feelings of unfairness and a perception that somehow 'other' social or cultural groups are getting more and are therefore a threat. The concept of dialogue lay at the heart of resolution strategies, through providing opportunities for segregated communities to mix and communicate and through the promotion of debate and consultation with young people with the purpose of 'engaging young people in the decision making process affecting their communities' (49). Young people are often positioned as being at the heart of community conflict and seen to be marginalised and without a voice. And since they are the upcoming generation of decision makers, it is argued that their voice needs to be listened to and included in community decisions, the aim being to empower young people to have a positive influence in transforming community conflict. Those in favour of Community Cohesion propose that it provides a framework for youth workers to create 'meaningful direct contact' between communities and also across territorial feuds that divide communities of the same ethnic origin (Thomas 2006, 48).

However, the agenda was contested. Counter arguments maintain that it doesn't tackle structural inequalities and is divisive. The Community Cohesion agenda sought to, 'establish a greater sense of citizenship based on a few common principles which are shared and observed by all sections of the community' (Cantle 2001, 10). Burnett (2004) argues that recommendations to celebrate cultures within a framework that establishes firm loyalty to the Nation are 'immediately problematic in that a commitment to shared national loyalty does not in any way begin to counter pre-existing structures of racial prejudice' (10). Furthermore, Green and Pinto (2005) state that 'multiculturalism [is] focused on celebrating differences, Community Cohesion concentrates on similarities and commonality' (49). Approaches to diversity that advocate cultural commonality can be seen to arise from the fear generated by events such as 9/11, leading to a 'war on terror' with its anti-difference and anti-Muslim focus. Worley (2005) points to, 'the increasingly hostile construction of asylum and immigration within the national imaginary' (489). This has led to increasing acceptance that people from Black and Minority Ethnic (BME) groups must adapt to fit with the cultural norms of the dominant society, with all its inequalities (Green and Pinto 2005, 50).

Contested approaches to dialogue

Dialogue is heralded as a potential means to resolve social conflict and assist democracy through its ability to communicate across difference and co-create new ways of understanding. However, the 'ideal of dialogue' has been challenged (Burbules 2000, 1). Democratic dialogue can be problematic as a result of historical oppressions and marginalisation of certain cultural groups, cultural values and beliefs. Spivak's (1988) influential essay 'Can the Subaltern Speak?' argues that the economically dispossessed cannot speak due to the inability of the colonial oppressor to hear and understand knowledge and perspectives other than through the lens of their own Western consciousness and values. Freire (1996) too argues that conversation thwarted by a power imbalance is not dialogue at all but rather indoctrination.

The issue of power and discourse in dialogue was debated in a series of exchanges between Gadamer and Habermas. Gadamer (1997) uses the metaphor of the horizon to describe the prejudices that we all bring to a conversation through which we have a limited 'horizon of understanding' (301). Through dialogue, we seek to increase our 'range of vision' that we see from a 'particular vantage point' (301). Gadamer (1997) sees conversational understanding as a process through which each person opens themselves to the other person and truly accepts their point of view as worthy of consideration. However, Habermas (1979) argues that distortion of meaning can occur in dialogue due to subtle yet powerful meanings that are often attached to words, and this can be used against the weaker partner by the more powerful. Nevertheless, in the 'Theory of Communicative Action', Habermas (1984) views language as a foundational component of society that can be used for coordinating action. Yet he distinguishes between two types of action: communicative action and strategic action. In communicative action, participants seek to achieve understanding and consensus, whereas in strategic action, participants seek practical success through pursuit of their own goals. Consequently, he proposes an 'ideal speech situation', whereby equality is sought and participants seek ways of identifying and exploring the distortions that exist. This holds similarities with Freire's (1996) notion of 'Conscientization', which refers to ways of raising the consciousness of communities and individuals in order that they can reconceptualise perceptions that they have previously understood as 'normal' or inevitable.

In *Pedagogy of the Oppressed*, Freire (1996) offers that, in terms of education for transformation, the essence of dialogue consists of two parts: reflection and action. He argues that reflection alone is 'verbalism' that is idle chatter that cannot lead to transformation. Action alone is 'activism' that becomes 'action for action's sake' (68–69).

Freire (1996) proposes that liberation cannot be bestowed on people as a gift but, rather, must be actively pursued. This involves a process of critical reflection whereby the oppressed come to recognise their dependency on their oppressors and move from being passive recipients of knowledge and ideas to being actively involved in the reconstruction of new ideas and democratic relationships that liberate both oppressed and oppressor. This paper explores ways in which young people have taken action through engaging in a social movement that utilises the arts to explore issues of conflict and oppression in their own communities and share their stories with other young people around the world. Habermas (1981) conceptualises new social movements as public struggles to regain forms of communicative action. Social movements based on communicative action can be seen as human-rights-based, rather than materialistic or economic-based movements, which seek to bring about changes in identity, culture and social understanding. Information is a crucial resource in modern society that plays a part in maintaining oppressive structures. As such, communicative action can serve as a form of resistance to influence the ways in which public discourse is structured, which is a necessary component of social change and hence conflict transformation.

Drawing on the arts as a form of dialogue

Arts approaches can mirror the strengths of verbal dialogue and reflect the limitations. However, as I will explore in this section, they have unique qualities, such as the ability to touch emotions, transcend verbal language barriers and promote creativity. Matarasso's (1997) extensive report, *The Social Impact of Participation in the Arts*, proposes:

> The greatest social impacts of participation in the arts arise from their ability to help people think critically about and question their experiences and those of others, not in a discussion group but with all the excitement, danger, magic, colour, symbolism, feeling, metaphor and creativity that the arts offer. (84)

The arts have been used to explore individual and collective narratives. Jupp (2006) offers that narratives are 'storied ways of knowing and communicating' (186). Storytellers forge connections between past, present and future by drawing on memories and reimagining more positive lives and futures. Lederach (1997) suggests:

> People need opportunity and space to express to and with one another the trauma of loss and their grief at that loss, and the anger that accompanies the pain and the memory of injustices experienced. ... Acknowledgement through hearing one another's stories validates experience and feelings and represents the first step towards restoration of the person and the relationship. (26)

Leitch (2008) proposes that visual imagery can powerfully evoke a storyline. She highlights way in which creative methods have been used to provide methods of 'safe expression' for strong, often negative, feelings, such as anger, frustration, indignation and rage. She draws on work carried out in Northern Ireland after 'the troubles', where a 'culture of silence' used as a coping mechanism had caused some young people to internalise fears and emotions (39). She suggests that individual and collective storytelling through poems and image making allowed the silence to be broken. Narratives of injustice that were previously 'unsayable', even 'unthinkable', were allowed to surface. This was said to provide a means for, 'marginal disenfranchised voices to articulate contributions towards change and systems of improvement for self and others' (48), which raises the question of whether such arts-based methods can disrupt silences, letting the subaltern speak (Spivak 1988).

Such methods use the arts to stimulate dialogue around troublesome issues. The non-verbal aspects of the arts play a major part in this process. Non-verbal messages can be depicted in ways that are universally understood. Lederach (2005) demonstrates this well in *The Moral Imagination*. He describes a peace process conference in Northern Ireland following 'the troubles' where a 'risk' had been taken to include a controversial artistic performance. This included traditional Irish dancers recruited from both sides of the conflict divide, a solo voice singing to a piano and a backdrop screen that played through visual images of 32 years of the troubles. Lederach explains:

> The song began and the dance troupe's graceful first steps brought hundreds in the audience to complete silence. The colour slides of Belfast's troubled murals, children running from fire bombs, funeral possessions and parades riveted the eyes and captured the haunted feel of the music and lyrics juxtaposed against the ballet-like movements of these young women dancing together though from different sides of the violent divide. The whole of the Irish conflict was held in a public space, captured in a moment that lasted fewer than five minutes. (2005, 153)

Lederach describes the impact of the performance, stating that several delegates were moved to silence and were wiping away tears. Looking back a decade later, he maintains that he cannot remember a single speech that happened on the day, however, he still remembers 'vividly the image and feelings of those five minutes of music, lyrics, choreography and photos' (153). He states, 'it created an echo in my head that has not gone away. It moved me' (153). The memorable and emotional powers of the arts are evident here. Duggan (1999) illuminates that emotions are important mechanisms that allow people to get in touch with their deeper feelings about issues of identity, violence and political change. Lederach (2005) offers that the arts used in this way can help us to 'return to our humanity' (154) and this is a necessary component of peace building. The non-verbal media of dance, music and visual image offered a message that could be understood, across cultures and languages, thereby answering Burbules's (2000) charge that dialogue can exclude when not everyone speaks the same language. Although this performance will hold greater socio-historic meaning locally, the underlying comment on the destruction of conflict juxtaposed against the creativity of culture has universal relevance.

However, as with all forms of knowing and understanding, the language of the arts can be context-specific, requiring verbal language to explain meaning across subjective boundaries. This becomes apparent through Augusto Boal's (1979) work in 'Theatre of the Oppressed'. Boal used theatre and photography to work with oppressed communities in South America. He explains a story where child workers agreed that a photograph of a nail on a wall symbolised 'exploitation'. The reason for this was not obvious to the adults present. The nail on a wall was the place where heavy equipment, used to clean shoes for money, was stored overnight. The children could not carry the heavy equipment home each night and were being charged much of their daily earnings for the rent of the nail by a businessman. For those children, the nail was therefore contextually symbolic of the concept of exploitation and became a pivotal point for exploring the issue in their lives. Whilst this highlights the need for verbal dialogue to accompany certain artistic media in order to communicate across subjective boundaries, as illustrated in the Lederach example, the arts also have the potential to transcend verbal language barriers and draw awareness to political and social conditions, promoting critical dialogue and enabling people to get in touch with their humanity (Lederach 2005). I now turn to the study on which this paper is based.

Painting the picture: diversity and conflict in rural south west England

The research that informed this paper took place in the city of Plymouth in the County of Devon, south west England. The area has developed rapidly over the last decade from a predominantly White[5] area to a more multicultural environment. Plymouth has been described as being based in one of the most homogenous areas in England (Burnett 2011). In the 2001 national census, it was stated that 1.6% of Plymouth's population was made up of people from BME communities, compared to 9.1% in the national population in England. However, by 2009, Plymouth's BME population had risen to approximately 9.1% (Burnett 2011). The demographic changes are in part due to development and expansion of the university and medical hospital, with increased recruitment from overseas. Plymouth also became part of the UK's Asylum Seeker programme that sought to disperse this group around the country to relieve pressure on London and the south east of England. Many communities struggled to adapt, resulting in an alarming number of racist incidents. The dispersal programme was accused of sending people into 'highly volatile environments', where they faced 'a worrying level of spontaneous racial harassment and racial attacks' due to 'entrenched views held by the host community against the incomers' (*The Independent*, 16 March 2007). This was especially high in the counties of Devon and Cornwall, where the research took place. The region was highlighted as the second most likely area in England to become a victim of racial crime (*Guardian*, 18 February 2001).

Although Plymouth is a city, rural issues are important here, with Plymouth being located within a predominantly rural area. Local research has documented the unique complexities of racism in rural Devon (Magne 2003). These range from acts of 'ignorance', to institutionalised racism, to overt race-hate crimes. Acts of ignorance are described as 'unwitting racism' due to 'lack of understanding' or 'mistaken beliefs' (Macpherson 1999). This can lead to unacknowledged racist stereotyping or patronising words or actions, regardless of an individual's good intentions, which can lead to 'institutional' discrimination that can exclude minority ethnic people from accessing professional services and being included within communities.

Considerable evidence of misconceptions, prejudice and racism are found to exist in rural areas and predominantly White areas, coupled with the assumption from White indigenous populations that racism is not a problem in such areas (Gaine 1987, 1995). The belief that resolving racism and intercultural conflict are not relevant in predominantly White areas is particularly problematic in the south west of England due to the prevalence of racial discrimination. Transforming intercultural conflict becomes complex when people either fear immigrant communities, don't believe racial conflict exists or are unaware that their actions and beliefs contribute to other people's exclusion. Hence, creative ways are called for to address the issue.

Illustrating the data: towards conflict transformation through arts-based dialogue

The ARROW programme took a creative approach to conflict transformation, utilising the arts as a language for sharing stories of conflict, oppression and injustice to promote critical dialogue between academics, practitioners and young people growing up in divided communities. It hosted a variety of events, including youth groups, arts-based conflict resolution workshops, intercultural exchanges, international symposiums, visiting theatre groups and a global congress. In their communities, young people took part in conflict-related projects, which were shared with other young people around the world online and during international visits and events.

Young people were recruited for Plymouth ARROW through partnerships with schools and through word of mouth. Being an ongoing programme, in existence since 2004, membership evolved and changed over time. In the Plymouth context, a predominantly White city, participants clustered between ages 13 to 18 years, being mostly White females from working-class and middle-class backgrounds, although young men and participants from different ethnic backgrounds also took part. In the early years of the ARROW programme, I worked in a voluntary capacity to help coordinate the Plymouth youth group. I was present at weekly sessions and became known by participants. During this time I held a focus-group session to explore their perceptions and experiences of involvement with the programme. At this time, the youth group consisted of 13 young people. These included 10 White females of whom two had a Black step-parent, one Black female, one Black male and one White male. Participants were given verbal and written information about the nature and purpose of the research and were given a voluntary option to take part. All participants chose to take part and gained signed parental consent. Names have been changed to preserve their anonymity. Fieldnotes were also kept during arts events and workshops and were reflected upon and incorporated as data. These include a week of arts activities between the Plymouth ARROW youth group and the visiting Durban, ARROW South Africa youth group and arts activities that took place during a UK ARROW congress held in Plymouth.

The focus-group session took place after the Durban youth group visit, but before the congress event. It was held as part of weekly youth group activities, to maintain continuity of process, yet delve deeper into participants' thoughts and experiences of the project. In keeping with ARROW ethos, the arts were incorporated into the research process. Duggan (1999) states, 'When people start talking through their painted images they are more in touch with their inner feelings because they produced the images' (341). The group were given sheets of paper and offered the choice to either write or draw in colour their experiences of being involved with ARROW. The purpose was to understand key experiences and junction points that acted as moments of growth or change. Participants were then invited to feed back to the whole group and discuss their writing or images and what they represented. The focus-group session was tape-recorded for analysis purposes and analysed thematically through clustering topics and issues raised by the participants. I highlight examples in the findings that reflect themes of the paper – these being, arts as a form of non-verbal dialogue, for transcending language barriers, promoting critical dialogue around issues of conflict, dispelling myths and stereotypes and transcending perceived barriers of difference. The results are to be understood within their context and endeavour to capture a particular issue of racial tension in a predominately White area of England and how the programme contributed to the transformation of participants' thinking in the early stages of the programme. Relevance can be found beyond the context in which the research took place due to the young people's experiences being representative of some other young people growing up in similar contexts. It is acknowledged that alternative perspectives and experiences may also exist which did not arise in this study.

Arts as form of non-verbal dialogue

In the spring of 2006, the ARROW youth group from Durban, South Africa, visited the Plymouth ARROW youth group for a week of arts-based activities. These included voice workshops, drama performances, forum theatre, a mask workshop, painting activities and storytelling. In the Plymouth context, this sought to address the destruction and discrimination in the south west of England caused by racist stereotypes and myths (Burnett 2011; Magne 2003), widen the horizons of young people growing up with little contact with diverse ethnic groups, and generate a movement for conflict transformation through bringing young people together from across the world. The Plymouth group consisted of predominantly White young people and it is on the voices of these young participants and their transforming conceptualisations of 'race' that the next section focuses. The visiting Durban ARROW group consisted of 16 Black young males and females aged 15 and 16 years.

In the lead up to the event, concerns were expressed from both groups on opposite sides of the world. Young White people in Plymouth asked questions such as 'will they be Black'[6] and 'will they speak English?' Whilst this can be interpreted as apprehension or inquisitiveness, literature on Whiteness and rural racism suggests that high levels of fear and misunderstandings exist due to negative media representations of Black and minority ethnic people, coupled with limited chance for these to be expelled due to lack of opportunity for White people in rural areas to mix with diverse cultures (Burnett 2011; Gaine 1987, 1995). The impact of the media is thus likely to have led to myths and stereotypes on both sides. Some parents of young people from the Durban ARROW youth group withdrew their children from the trip due to beliefs about terrorism in the UK, fearing it was not safe to travel following reports of terrorism in the news. In contrast, the Plymouth group had not considered terrorism, at this time, due to the city's far distance from London where previous terrorist activity had taken place. In Plymouth, fears centred more on fear of 'difference' and this led to stereotyping, misunderstandings and social exclusion for many BME people living in the area (Burnett 2011; Magne 2003). Focus-group data supported this notion. Speaking about the first day of events following the arrival of the Durban youth group, one participant stated:

> That day I made lots of friends. Before that day I was like apprehensive because I thought oh I hope we don't have segregation ... but it was like so friendly as soon as we were there we were like talking and it was like whoosh! At lunch there was no majority in the groups of the tables because

everyone wanted to talk to all the different people and were really interested. (Joe, White male, age 15)

Here, Joe acknowledges the issue of segregation, suggesting it is a common problem from the Plymouth perspective. Curiously, although participants had joined the youth group wanting to get involved in dialogue with diverse communities around the world, fears of 'the other' were nevertheless present. Joe also expresses the impact of the dialogic approach through the comment 'it was like whoosh!' This described the speed at which perceived barriers had been lifted, enabling the groups to become 'really interested' in listening to one another. The arts techniques that aided this reaction will be illustrated later. Further participants described the changes in perspective that took place:

It was completely different to how I thought it would be, I thought they would not be able to speak English well, but that was their first language. (Roshelle, White female, age 15)

They read all the same magazines as us, they knew all the same bands as us, it was like Oh!! (Sarah, White female, age 14)

They were so similar to us but they had a different life to us. (Charlotte, White female, age 14)

The first quote reveals the dispelling of stereotypes. It shows Roshelle's starting assumption was that South Africans do not speak English well because they speak another language. She shows that her expectations had changed and her previous beliefs about 'African'[7] people had been 'completely different'. Equally, in the second quote, Sarah demonstrates a change in perspective that appears to have dismantled previously held stereotypes about 'African' people. The tone at the end of Sarah's comment, 'it was like Oh!' suggests a prior belief that people in South Africa and people in England have fundamentally different cultural influences and that it came as quite a surprise to find out how similar some of their cultural influences were. Curiously, the knowledge of each other's musical tastes arrived, not through organised discussion but through the Durban group giving an impromptu demonstration of a local cultural dance, to which the Plymouth group joined in and responded with a dance to a current song they knew. This led to an excited exchange of dance moves and songs and the recognition that they shared much in common. The third quote by Charlotte offers recognition that the two groups had both similarities and differences. This point reflects back to Gallagher and Pritchard's (2007) contention regarding assimilation and multiculturalism and whether we are seeking 'elevation of similarity' or 'celebration of difference' (567). The three quotes, coupled with Joe's comment about fears of segregation, appear to reveal relief when examined against apprehension that existed prior to the two groups meeting. Whilst it is evident that stereotypes that lead to 'fear of the other' have been challenged, the point of contention here is whether participants felt relief that they now perceived 'the other' as similar to themselves, thus reinforcing a notion of 'we are all the same', or whether they felt able to celebrate and enjoy differences. Both are important. Finding commonality offers a starting point for challenging stereotypes and building relationships across previously perceived boundaries (Lederach 1997). However, it is in the widening out of experience and horizons (Gadamer 1997), seeing beyond one's own context, that inclusivity can be found. Some participants highlighted the global nature of the programme that provided opportunities for contact with cultures around the world and helped expand their understanding of their relationship in the world:

> Being part of a bigger group, it's a worldwide group so I feel like I'm part of something greater than just my little community; it's the world community. It helps me get in touch ... we have our small community in Plymouth and there is also the wider community that is the world. (Joe, White male, age 15)

> Meeting the South Africans was amazing ... when the South Africa group came I felt the whole world was getting the ARROW vibe. (Riana, White female, age 15)

The first comment suggests that conceptualising belonging to a global community helps remove the feeling of segregation, leading to a sense of feeling 'in touch'. This is further reflected in the second quote through the idea of creating worldly connections. Riana's quote expresses elation at meeting the South African group – again demonstrating a change in perception from anxiety about 'the other' to excitement regarding a sense of connection to the rest of the world. The idea of 'the ARROW vibe' relates to a feeling of connectedness to the world and stands in contrast to comments made prior to the event, where young people felt separated by aspects of difference such as skin colour and language.

This highlights where young people were at and the changes that took place. One might argue that simply bringing diverse cultures together could lead to changes in perspectives about each other. However, this is not necessarily the case. Green and Pinto (2005) note that due to the real extent of racism in the UK, even when cross-cultural events are organised, people don't tend to mix:

> People don't tend to mix, even if you organised a big community wide event people wouldn't mix ... Asians get separated, blacks get separated, whites get separated. (Voice of young person speaking about community cohesion, cited in Green and Pinto 2005, 54)

The arts were seen to have a specific role in the breaking down of barriers between the Plymouth and Durban youth groups. The morning began with two groups sitting on separate sides of the room. The atmosphere was strained. Young people from both sides later expressed their fears about the other based on stereotypes and limited, yet negative, media reporting about each other's countries. The groups were brought together through a voice workshop. This involved chanting and harmonising as a whole group, followed by voice recognition activities where young people were paired with a partner from the other youth group, and had to all find each other across a room, with eyes closed, using simple voice call rhythms rather than words. Dialogue took the form of voice, yet no language was privileged through the activity, because it was based on sound not language. Spivak (1988) argues that truly engaging with the subaltern involves removing oneself as 'expert' in a binary social relationship of 'them' and 'us'. Non-verbal arts media offer a form of emotional communication that potentially disrupts divisive hierarchies in the moment. After the activity, both groups began to speak to each other. There was an air of excitement in the room. Conversations were fast and loud. Young people were laughing and chatting with one another, seeking to find out more about each other. They could be heard enquiring what music they liked, what dances they knew. In groups they broke into impromptu song as they recognised they knew much of the same music. They began to dance and share dance routines that they knew. They began teaching each other dances from their own countries. The events facilitators and arts practitioners stood back and watched, whilst the young people transformed their relationships with one another. Here, arts-based communication can be seen to provide methods of 'safe expression' that moved past internalised fears, emotions and concerns, thereby disrupting the silence and bringing diverse people together. The activity appears to reflect Leitch's (2008) proposal that the arts can act as a medium for breaking the silence where young voices have been oppressed.

Whilst a number of arts activities took place during the week, including painting, dance, drama and storytelling, there is not room here to discuss the full range of activities. What I illustrate through this example is the potential of the arts as a form of non-verbal dialogue for transcending perceived barriers of difference. It must be noted here that young people involved in these activities were not in conflict with one another *per se* due to living on opposite sides of the globe. However, breaking down perceived barriers of difference in a workshop context can potentially lead to the breaking down of such stereotypes, barriers and hostile behaviour towards people previously perceived as 'other' in their own communities due to changes in perceptions of diversity. Movements in perception are said to occur through emotional engagement that is elicited through the arts (Duggan 1999) and through aspects such as excitement, magic, colour and metaphor that the arts offer (Matarasso 1997, 84). One young person described a feeling of 'spiritual connection' during the voice workshop that promoted a feeling of being bonded with the new group. Such non-verbal forms of communication offer alternative ways of learning about the world through making internal emotional shifts to which new meaning can be attached. This mirrors Lederach's (1997) theory of conflict transformation that moves beyond focus on conflict issues to creative methods that focus on relationship building. Such 'communicative action' (Habermas 1984) can be seen as a form of human-rights based action that seeks to disrupt negative narratives of difference that contribute to racial conflict. I now turn to the role of the arts for promoting critical dialogue around more troublesome issues.

Arts-based critical dialogue through storytelling

In the summer of 2009, a UK ARROW Congress was held in Plymouth. The congress provided an opportunity for young people to come together, from a variety of youth groups around the UK, to share practice, talk about the challenges faced in their own areas and contexts and learn from one another, offering ways that they use the arts to tackle difficult issues in their communities. Youth groups came from Burnley, Derry, Durham, Plymouth and Slough. The young people present formed a diverse group in terms of gender, age, culture, ethnicity, heritage, ability, disability and religious background. Ages ranged from 13 to 25 years, including young people of English, Ghanaian, Indian, Irish, Jamaican, Malaysian, Pakistan and Saudi Arabian heritage. In addition, a wide range of experiences were present due to participants coming from communities that had very different histories, including the history of 'the troubles' in Derry, Northern Ireland, and the 'race riots' in Burnley in the north of England. The groups shared, through drama and dance, stories of the troublesome contexts in which they are growing up. Metaphor, action, movement and emotion were utilised as mediums to communicate issues affecting their lives. Issues included stereotyping, racial and religious discrimination, divided communities, competitive group behaviour and territorial conflict. The arts activities were used to describe, explore, pose questions, trigger empathy and promote critical dialogue around the issues.

However, the approach is not without controversy. It was observed that when diverse peoples are brought together, they bring their own collections of fears, stereotypes, myths and discriminatory attitudes and behaviour. As such, conflicts of interest could be seen to emerge amongst participants. In a diverse group, the problem emerges regarding whose issues are prioritised and tackled. A danger exists that dominant voices may obscure more marginalised voices (Spivak 1988), leading to the prioritising of their issues rather than the addressing of their prejudices. For example, a young Black male, experiencing racial discrimination, spoke in ways that were stereotypical and derogatory towards women. And the voice of a young Black female, who protested about the use of a word that she considered offensive towards Black people, was 'silenced' by White participants who, unable to relate to her experience, made humour out of the incident in an endeavour to discharge the awkwardness of the situation. Ledwith (1997) argues that people may be both recipients and perpetrators of oppression, yet may be unaware of how their actions disadvantage or marginalise others. The problem is therefore in recognising that addressing conflict involves challenging oneself as well as others and this can cause discomfort. The alternative is keeping things superficial and easy, which serves little purpose in creating social change. This raises the question of engagement, when people feel they may get blamed and criticised. Participants mentioned that people won't engage when they fear they 'might get jumped upon'. Further conversations revealed a reluctance to work with what are perceived as someone else's issues when they have their own issues. However, one arts practitioner explained a way of conceptualising a solution:

> Understanding issues that are coming from other's experiences not your own generally involve a journey not an explanation and this takes a period of time to explore, digest, absorb, grow and develop ... (George, White male)

Here, George acknowledges that social change is a process that involves connecting with other people's experiences in ways beyond superficial explanations or dialogue about their troubles, which may cause discomfort due to a sense of feeling blamed. Young people explained potential ways in which the arts techniques helped traverse barriers of disengagement:

> It doesn't put the audience on the spot because they can just sit there and watch and think in their own minds, and with the forum theatre instead of just standing there saying what do you guys think, rather say how would you like to have changed what you just saw. (Roshelle, White female, age 15)

> I think the role play helps. There is nothing that can change your opinion more than being the person that you're against. (Sarah, White female, age 14)

> It helps you think outside the box about what's going on outside, not just in your little box but in the entire world. (Charlotte, White female, age 14)

Roshelle seems to suggest that the artistic media offers a method for entering the conversation through play, allowing issues to be explored in creative ways that are less intimidating than they might otherwise be when tackled directly. The implication being that participants can explore creative ways to change the story being told, which may trigger internal changes in perception. Liebmann (1996) furthers this understanding, offering the arts can help 'develop strategies for handling external conflicts, this is intimately connected with internal conflict ... much of the work undertaken is to resolve inner conflicts and thus influence external events' (5). Sarah implies that engaging with theatre as a means of exploring different people's perspectives of an issue can lead to personal change and renewed ways of thinking about an issue. Her comment points to the language of the arts as a way to evoke empathy with 'the other'. Charlotte reveals that the process of sharing stories through the arts helped with expanding perceptions to include others. This suggests movement beyond concern with one's own story to recognising 'what's going on' for other people. Gadamer's (1997) metaphor of the horizon is relevant here, although in this case demonstrating that not just verbal dialogue but also arts-based dialogue increases one's 'range of vision' (143). Charlotte's notion of thinking outside the box has two meanings: the promotion of critical thinking around issues of racial conflict and expanding one's perception beyond one's immediate local context. The comment reflects Matarasso's (1997) statement that the arts help promote critical thinking and creativity, thereby helping people to question their own and others' experiences.

If we return to Lederach's (2005, 53) description that the arts can create 'an echo' that moves people and does not go away, we see that the emotional impact of the arts can trigger new internal ways of understanding social issues that contribute to conflict. Potentially, this can help people move to new places of understanding that they might otherwise have disengaged from due to issues being difficult. Lederach (1997) proposes it is in the sharing and hearing of one another's stories, experiences and feelings that our experiences feel validated and this helps with restoring oneself and with the rebuilding of relationships with others, and these are necessary aspects of peace building.

Conclusion

This paper explores the role of the arts as a complement to dialogue for peace building. Dialogic pedagogy is championed for its abilities to assist democracy (Freire 1996) and transform conflicts through building human relationships and developing new understandings (Lederach 1997). However, issues of power, voice and language exist, whereby more powerful groups are said to dominate perspectives and set agendas rendering the least powerful groups unable to speak (Spivak 1988). As such, dialogue is criticised for its inability to tackle structural inequalities that lead to discrimination, disadvantage and poverty. Nevertheless, Freire (1996) argues that dialogic pedagogy can be liberating – through a process of action and reflection, individuals can analyse their own reality and become aware of distorted perceptions and take action to bring about social changes. The ARROW programme, now the INDRA congress, brings together young people to take action to transform conflict in their communities around the world. In many cases, young people are growing up in deeply divided communities with complex societies and troubled histories. The programme does not purport to resolve such embedded complexities. However, the work can be seen as promoting a human-rights agenda, which is a necessary component of social change. Habermas (1981) highlights that human rights social movements, based on communicative action, can bring about changes in identity, culture and social understandings through resisting public discourse that plays a part in maintaining oppressive social structures.

In the Plymouth context, young people's perceptions of being part of a 'worldwide' cultural group were significant. Membership of ARROW helped participants to conceptualise the world beyond their own local context, envisioning their place in the wider world, thereby broadening their 'horizon of understanding' (Gadamer 1997, 301). This appeared to challenge previous stereotypes and conceptualisations of 'the other'. However, the data reveal the existence of dichotomous ways of seeing other cultures as either 'not like us' or 'just like us'. This is potentially problematic in that focus is placed on distinctions of difference rather than individual aspects with similarities and differences amongst us all. When speaking about multiculturalism versus assimilation, Gallagher and Pritchard (2007) question whether, if a return to assimilation occurs, 'elevation of similarity and commonality may be given precedence over the celebration of difference' (567). I question here whether young people growing up under an assimilation framework might be affected by fears about difference rather than an enjoyment of celebrating diversity. This is an issue that further research might uncover.

The arts enabled communication beyond words, in visual and emotional ways that young people described as being exciting, motivational, spiritual and bonding, thus helping create relationships across previously perceived boundaries. Leitch (2008) offers that individual and collective storytelling through poems and image making allowed previously silenced narratives of injustice to be articulated. Young people suggested the use of the arts enabled them to engage with serious issues in playful, non-threatening ways, which offered a way to bridge the gap between engaging and disengaging when issues were perceived as troublesome. In the incidences described, participants had a common language, however, arts media offers potential for working across language barriers. Lederach (2005) suggests the visual and emotional impacts of arts performances can move people in lasting ways. The languages of signs and symbols can be utilised in ways that transcend language barriers, prompting an internal critique. Lederach (2005) theorises, 'the artistic process initially breaks beyond what can be rationally understood and then returns to a place of understanding that may analyse, think it through, and attach meaning to it' (160). Thus, stories told through arts activities can offer descriptions or explanations of given situations and this can open up issues for exploration through further critical dialogue. They can also provide a method for visiting each other's experiences and living a moment of each other's lives through visual image and performance. It was explained that real experiences are important and tapping into people's experiences helps to create empathy.

However, the study must be placed in context. Although the data suggest that arts-based dialogue can encourage young people to engage in critical dialogue about issues of conflict and help remove barriers caused by stereotypes and myths, the data do not reveal the extent to which it can deal with overt race-hate crime carried out by those with embedded racist attitudes. This is a serious issue in the south west of England (Magne 2003). Further study is needed to explore the ability for arts-based dialogue to transform conflict at this level. The data focus on the experiences of the Plymouth youth group and therefore is limited in its ability to explore alternative perspectives and experiences that may have arisen from participants from the global youth groups. The data do not extend to long-term effects of the programme and therefore further research is needed to examine to what extent and in what ways learning continues beyond the immediate context in which it takes place. Nevertheless, this paper offers that arts-based dialogue can complement verbal dialogue through its ability to transcend verbal language barriers, allow previously silenced narratives to be articulated and encourage people to think critically about themselves, humanity and the world.

Notes

1. In the UK the term Black has been used as a political term to refer to individuals and community groups who are not White and who face disadvantage and discrimination.
2. A list of partner organisations can be found at http://www.theindracongress.com/partners.php
3. Information about Al Harah Theatre's partnership with the INDRA congress can be found at http://www.alharah.org/index.php?option=com_content&view=article&id=46&Itemid=187&lang=en
4. Information about ARROW South Africa can be found at http://coh.ukzn.ac.za/CentreforCommunication-Media-Society_copy1/ARROW.aspx
5. Literature on 'whiteness' argues 'white' skin affords people a privileged position in society, yet this privilege is rarely recognised by White people themselves, who often conceptualise their Whiteness as 'normality'. Nevertheless, this in turn leads to a positioning of 'superiority', with 'non-White' people being judged against Whiteness as the 'norm'.
6. In this context the term Black refers to people who have brown skin. The author recognises that terminology and meanings differ around the world.
7. The author recognises the immense diversity of peoples in Africa. However, the term 'African' is used to highlight a common misconception amongst people growing up in predominantly White areas in the UK, where non-White people are often perceived as a homogenised group.

References

Boal, Augusto. 1979. *Theatre of the Oppressed*. London: Pluto Press.
Burbules, Nicholas C. 2000. "The Limits of Dialogue as a Critical Pedagogy." In *Revolutionary Pedagogies: Cultural Politics, Instituting Education, and the Discourse of Theory*, edited by Peter Trifonas, 251–273. London: Routledge.
Burnett, J. 2004. "Community Cohesion and the State." *Race and Class Journal* 45 (3): 1–18.

Burnett, Jon. 2011. *The New Geographies of Racism*. London: Institute of Race Relations.

Cantle, E. 2001. *Community Cohesion: A Report of the Independent Review Team*. London: HMSO.

Duggan, Dave. 1999. "Arts Approaches to the Conflict in Northern Ireland." In *Arts Approaches to Conflict*, edited by Marian Liebmann, 335–346. London: Jessica Kingsley.

Freire, Paulo. 1996. *Pedagogy of the Oppressed*. London: Penguin Books.

Gadamer, H.-G. 1997. *Truth and Method*. 2nd ed. New York: Continuum.

Gaine, Chris. 1987. *No Problem Here*. London: Hutchinson.

Gaine, Chris. 1995. *Still No Problem Here*. London: Trentham Books.

Gallagher, Tony, and Rosalind Pritchard. 2007. "Assimilation and Multiculturalism: Evolving Conceptual Frameworks." *Compare: A Journal of Comparative and International Education* 37 (5): 567–576.

Green, R., and R. Pinto. 2005. "Youth Related Community Cohesion. Policy and Practice: The Divide between Rhetoric and Reality." *Youth and Policy Journal* 88 (Summer): 45–61.

Habermas, Jürgen. 1979. *Communication and the Evolution of Society*. Translated by T. McCarthy. London: Heinemann.

Habermas, Jürgen. 1981. "New Social Movements." *Telos* 49: 33–37.

Habermas, Jürgen. 1984. *Theory of Communicative Action Volume One*. Cambridge, MA: Beacon Press.

Jupp, Victor, ed. 2006. *The Sage Dictionary of Social Research Methods*. London: Sage.

Lederach, John Paul. 1997. *Building Peace: Sustainable Reconciliation in Divided Societies*. Washington, DC: United States Institute of Peace Press.

Lederach, John Paul. 2005. *The Moral Imagination: The Art and Soul of Building Peace*. Oxford: Oxford University Press.

Ledwith, Margaret. 1997. *Participating in Transformation: Towards a Model of Community Empowerment*. Birmingham: Venture Press.

Leitch, Ruth. 2008. "Creatively Researching Children's Narratives through Images and Drawings." In *Doing Visual Research with Children and Young People*, edited by Pat Thomson, 37–58. London: Routledge.

Liebmann, Marian, ed. 1996. *Arts Approaches to Conflict*. London: Jessica Kingsley.

Macpherson, William. 1999. *The Stephen Lawrence Inquiry*. London: The Stationery Office.

Magne, Sam. 2003. *Multi Ethnic Devon: A Rural Handbook: Experiencing and Coping with Racism*. Exeter: Devon REC.

Matarasso, François. 1997. *Use or Ornament? The Social Impact of the Arts*. Stroud: Commedia.

Spivak, Gayatri. 1988. "Can the Subaltern Speak?" In *Marxism and the Interpretation of Culture*, edited by Cary Nelson and Lawrence Grossberg, 271–313. Urbana: University of Illinois Press.

Thomas, P. 2006. "The Impact of Community Cohesion on Youth Work: A Case Study from Oldham." *Youth and Policy Journal* 93: 41–60.

Worley, C. 2005. "It's Not about Race. It's about the Community." *Critical Social Policy Journal* 25 (4): 483–496.

Lebanese youth narratives: a bleak post-war landscape

Roseanne Saad Khalaf

Department of English and Creative Writing, American University of Beirut, Beirut, Lebanon

To identify the themes that define the lives of a generation living in a conflict-ridden post-war society, I explore the changing views of Lebanese students through an analysis of the personal narrative texts that they created during my creative writing workshops over a 16-year period (1997–2012). Increasingly, young Lebanese feel trapped in a violent past, a threatening present and a hopeless future. As traditional forms of stability and loyalty (family and state) become more dysfunctional, modern alternative sources of education, employment, security and public discourse remain absent, creating an ever-widening disjunction between expectations and disheartening lived realities. Since 1998, student texts have focused on three salient thematic groupings: Idealism (1998–2005), Activism (2005–2008) and, most recently, Disillusionment (2008–present). In an atmosphere of escalating intolerance and hostility, it is hardly surprising that students are currently escaping to spaces of indulgence and personal gratification. As ongoing regional conflicts fuel local sectarian rivalries, I argue that reengaging educated young Lebanese in non-confrontational narratives that challenge dysfunctional systems can play a vital role in disrupting a dangerous sectarian narrative that is fast threatening to entangle Lebanon in yet another brutal war.

Introduction

This paper is a reflexive, exploratory study into the changing views of Lebanese students at the American University of Beirut (AUB), a post-war, post-memory generation, from Lebanon's diverse religious, political and social groups, who have participated in my creative writing workshops over a period of 16 years (1997–2012). Their discussions and narratives are shaped by intense lived experiences that draw heavily from family, social settings and political circumstances. In this fast-shifting terrain of escalating social ills and sectarian violence, students feel increasingly trapped in a violent, unresolved past, threatening present and hopeless future.

Although the narratives crafted by my students are characterised by different writing styles and distinctive voices, they typify the views of young people who have moved beyond a previously explored terrain that existed during and immediately after the 2005 Lebanese Youth *Intifada*. Today, prospects of a more tolerant, plural and diverse political and social culture are fast fading. The futility of efforts to restore trust and dialogue in a country plagued by unresolved conflict and unappeased hostility makes students uninterested in becoming change makers engaged in the crafting of a new political culture. Instead, they are desensitising from traumatic events both internally and regionally, while rejecting any form of public discourse, civic engagement and participatory democracy. An escalating frenzy to indulge in pleasurable activities by cultivating spaces for self-gratification has become evident. Currently, the most striking narrative theme focuses on having as much fun as possible while planning exit strategies from a country that has so cunningly and successfully silenced youthful voices.

With the 1990 Taif Accord, the Lebanese Civil War was officially brought to a close and post-war Lebanon was optimistically perceived as a period when the violence that pervaded almost two decades of strife could be forgotten, leaving the Lebanese to focus on reconstruction, reconciliation and revamping a decaying political system. Yet none of the issues that instigated the war have been adequately addressed. Crucial questions regarding inter-communal conflict, accountability of wartime atrocities and nation building continue to be conveniently ignored. On February 14, 2005, the brutal killing of Prime Minister Rafic Hariri and the subsequent string of political assassinations and disquieting public protests that followed Syria's withdrawal, threw the country into further disarray. A year later, the devastating 2006 summer Israel-Hezbollah War intensified feelings of hate and hostility between sectarian groups. Currently, these tensions are being fuelled by regional conflicts, particularly the spillover from Syria's relentless civil war.

Throughout this long, turbulent post-war period, and in direct response to the unfolding political circumstances, participants in my AUB workshops engaged in insightful conversations. To best explore relevant concerns, I engaged in close readings of students' personal narratives in 25 creative writing sections from 1997 to 2012, before applying narrative analysis to isolate salient and recurring themes. The themes constituted three distinct categories: *Idealism* (1997–2005), *Activism* (2005–2008) and *Disillusionment* (2008–Present). Although each of the three is analysed separately alongside narrative excerpts to capture the shifting voices of students over the years, my paper explores the latter in more detail. It touches only briefly on the first two since they have been the focus of previous publications, most recently, *Youthful Voices in Post-war Lebanon* (Khalaf 2009) and *Idealistic and Indignant Young Lebanese* (in Khalaf and Khalaf 2011).

Dozens of conversations and debates were recorded during workshop sessions.

Literature review

Recent studies on Lebanese youth have elucidated specific attributes and behaviour associated with and resulting from a troubled post-war setting. In 'Between Silences and Screams' (2011) Craig Larkin concentrates on the post-war generation of Lebanese youth trapped between conflicting forces of collective memory and collective amnesia. Drawing on Marianne Hirsch's concept of *Postmemory* (Hirsh 1997, 1998), he examines the memory of a generation struggling with narrative accounts of events that preceded their birth. Bereft of meaningful narratives to explain Lebanon's post-war realities, young people remain unable to reconcile their past in order to live for their future. Larkin's findings correspond to the concerns of my students during the earlier post-war years (1997–2005), when the most striking themes explored feelings of marginality and entrapment, being abandoned in a country characterised by a violent past they could neither understand nor come to terms with.

In the aftermath of the brutal assassination of Rafic Hariri in 2005, my students quickly became involved in the surge of political activism calling for participatory democracy and reform. Many joined the Youth *Intifada*, demanding that Syrian forces leave Lebanon, calling for the resignation of the Lebanese government and the revamping of a dysfunctional political system. Of course those who joined March 8 had a different political agenda but were equally vocal and active in demanding change. The consequences of such momentous mobilisation on reshaping the collective identity of Lebanese youth (Gahre 2011) were immense. Initially, despite diverse backgrounds and ideological leanings, involvement in the uprising heightened national consciousness and the primacy of Lebanese identity among youthful groups. However, two years on, the youthful enthusiasm that had inspired the massive mobilisation was derailed by self-serving politicians, along with future prospects of a more tolerant, plural and diverse political culture.

During subsequent years, my students' gaze shifted inward, blocking out the dangerous sectarian Lebanese narrative and the desire to formulate strategies against the rigidities of confessional politics. By 2008, bold themes of defiance began to take shape: recreation, pleasure, self-indulgence, having fun and emigration.

Current research suggests that they are not alone in seeking pleasure spaces of indulgence. Such hedonistic activities are perhaps a way to defy the battleground that Lebanon can so quickly become. Nicolien Kegels (2011), in her study on nightlife in times of war, focuses on a group of Lebanese upper-class young adults before and during the July 2006 Israeli war on Lebanon. Upper-class nightclubs, Kegel argues, become one of the best places to show off riches because they are designed to optimise flaunting wealth and confirming social status. Despite the devastating war, leisure, conspicuous consumption and an excessive display of privileges continued to define the lifestyle of this group of young Lebanese.

Much like Mahdavi's (2011) argument that 'having fun' in Iran is a direct challenge to the moral paradigm of the regime and a way for young people to assert their agency against its restrictions, my students are carving out pleasure spaces, not only as acts of defiance but to escape the never-ending political tensions and ills alongside the overwhelming sense of helplessness due to circumstances beyond their control. As they assume bolder stances, daring personal stories of desire and gratification are starting to map a radically different, more fluid (Bauman 2000) landscape. Strictures aiming to silence, uphold moral judgment or hypocrisy; mindsets seeking to control private lives are presently fiercely contested and ignored.

Methodology and content

This paper explores the changing views and attitudes in the personal narrative texts of AUB students who have participated in my creative writing workshops over a 16-year period (1997–2012). Although my sample comes from a private university, efforts in recent years have greatly enlarged the pool of unrestricted financial aid to ensure that students in need of financial support are not turned away. Consequently, my students increasingly reflect Lebanon's diverse socio-economic and religious composition: Christian, Druze, Shiia and Sunni Muslims.

Nonfiction workshops are held over a 14-week period (one semester) and consist of 15 students, between the ages of 18 and 21, men and women from numerous academic disciplines, meeting once a week for two and a half hours to focus on discussing required readings, crafting narrative texts and self-expression outside the strictures and constraints otherwise present in mainstream Lebanese society.

Quite often, my students become 'imprisoned' by their own stories (Gill 2009), unable to escape a given script, or boundaries resulting from barriers imposed by family, religion, culture, personal trauma and other forces seemingly beyond their control. Understandably, stories of devastation and pain or ancestral memories may unconsciously influence their narratives (Asseily 2009). Pain's inexpressibility, its ability to destroy language (Scarry 1985), can make the narrative process exceedingly slow, riddled with silences, stops and starts. Negotiating this essential struggle (Goodson 2009) through the 'narrative maze' requires a sensitive process of de-stabilising and re-stabilising (Goodson and Gill forthcoming 2014) that is necessary for awareness and transformation.

Openly exploring complex, volatile issues, deep inner feelings and personal views can be a daunting experience in a diverse classroom setting defined by strong views and differences. Creating spaces for honest discussions and critical debate is possible because our *contact zone* remains protected from the threatening outside gaze by the *safety net* of our classroom, where critical exchanges that deal with difference serve primarily to instigate debate and broaden awareness in a tolerant academic setting. Our autonomous *comfort zone* becomes a participatory *contact zone*, where conflicting attitudes are openly addressed and awareness heightened through imaginative text creation and critical discourse. To protect confidentially, real names have been changed. Reassuring students that strict anonymity will be observed creates an atmosphere of trust and an eagerness to share moving personal stories.

In my workshops, the importance of context anchored in Lebanon is paramount. Instead of constantly 'filling up' the curriculum, I encourage students to draw freely from day-to-day lived experiences alongside what is occurring locally, regionally and globally. In relocating the personal within broader cultural and political contexts, students move from that which seems completely private to broader historic and political contexts (Kamler 2001). Soon, personal experiences begin to enter into a realm of shared discourse that is wider and more social than that which characterises the individual.

As a result, workshops are guided and informed by a basic premise: how to use narratives – articulated in an uncensored classroom setting – to shed light on broader socio-cultural and political transformations. To make seemingly marginal and private matters become closely connected to broader societal transformations so that individual stories start to form a collective narrative of a larger journey through linkages of particular cases (Ewick and Silbey 1995). Apart from defining the views of a new generation, texts highlight significant youth experiences outside the hegemonic influences of public transcripts (Boym 1996). They provide counter-narratives, digressions and detours from the dominant story or accepted biography of a fast-changing post-war society.

Although the findings of my study represent the views of students in the *comfort zone* of workshops at an elitist university, the significance of the results, limited as they may seem, should not be undermined. Even marginal views, when given voice, inevitably begin to circulate in the mainstream where they are taken into account and recorded (Pinar 1997). Finally, the author acknowledges the limitations of this reflexive, exploratory study, resulting from the potential for bias on my part. Intentionally, I have not adhered to the notion that scholarly writers should erase their voices from the work they produce. Because I share the lived experiences of my students, it is near impossible to work silently on the sidelines (Charmaz and Mitchell 1997).

Idealism

In 1995, upon returning to Lebanon and AUB after an absence of 10 years, it became evident that my returnee students harboured feelings of 'between-ness', marginality, hybridity and exclusion alongside idealistic dreams of instigating change. The difficulties required in adjusting to a scarred, fragmented and highly unstable post-war society, unable to come to terms with its turbulent past, were immense. Although the 1992 Tiaf Agreement officially brought the Lebanese War to a close, young Lebanese remained devoid of war memory, trapped in the pain resulting from over a decade of protracted violence. Worse still, competing memories and stories complicated the confusion. The post-modernity experience of fragmented (Giddens 1991) and non-unitary (Bloom 1996) identities, of living in multiple places, in between cultures and juggling hybrid identities was a condition my students had clearly internalised.

The re-entry of young Lebanese who, together with their parents, had temporarily relocated abroad to escape the dangers of the Lebanese War, became a hugely complex and sensitive process. Issues of reconciliation and nation building, attempts to understand and move beyond the pain of the past were persistent and recurring themes during our weekly workshops:

> I remember the way my mother used to speak of this country, eyes downcast, trembling voice, as though the words threatened to choke her. She would speak of a time before war as though in a distant dream, as though the country had never witnessed demolition and spilled blood. (Alyan 2006, 192)

Students challenged the pervasive conspiracy of silence, the nostalgic attitudes and collective amnesia embraced by so many older Lebanese:

> My parents avoid talking about the Lebanese War. They refuse to discuss the violence that destroyed their 'perfect' country. They dwell in a make-believe land where the real past is completely obliterated. (Hanan)

Students struggled with conflicting pre-war accounts as no national or collective narrative exists. When asked about the war, they became confused, even bewildered: 'I have never known the reasons behind the Lebanese War. When I ask I get many contradictory answers,' Hussein movingly explains. Rana feels the same way: 'I don't know much about the war, in fact barely anything. Rarely has anyone told me stories about it. My family never mentions it. Still, it hurts to know that the war happened.' Leila feels betrayed by Lebanon:

> My country has beautiful scenery, perfect weather and wonderful food. It should be the ideal place to live but it's not. It's a sad and dangerous place. I opened my eyes to the final phase of a war that I never understood: a war that I consider to be useless. How can I feel I belong to a country that has caused me so much pain? (Leila)

Caught in fragmented, inconsistent, often irreconcilable scripts, students during this period eagerly explored issues of identity and belonging and grappled with ways to understand a bitter war, in order to embrace new possibilities. During the writing of *Transit Beirut: New Writing and Images* (Halasa and Khalaf 2004) the post-war period seemed to me an exciting, promising time when the war-torn past and subsequent regeneration made Lebanon unique among contemporary Arab countries. The legacy of violence, alongside the resilience it created were powerful factors in the search for a new Lebanese identity, shaped through public discourse and civic engagement.

Initially, my returnee students felt the same way. It was refreshing to witness their determination to challenge rigid strictures imposed by those who had decided to safeguard inflexible ways of thinking. Students were not potentates guarding territory or upholding tradition. They exemplified Edward Said's (1991) notion of a traveller who depends not on power but on motion and a willingness to go into different worlds to experience constant displacements and interruptions to keep views from solidifying (Bauman 2000), thus reinforcing a state of post-modern hybridity, openness and a restless opposition to all orthodoxies.

During this time, class discussions and narratives focused relentlessly on the tensions caused by this invisible conflict but also on a deep desire for change. There was a refreshing sense of optimism:

> We are constantly put in a tug-of-war situation because we are a challenge, a silent invasion against unreasonable and enforced traditional values and ideas. Actually, we're a wake-up call that needs to be heeded before it's too late. (Nabil)

> It seems like people in Lebanon have spent decades resisting change. They use the excuse of tradition and outmoded values to ensure control. (Suha)

> I know we can create a new and improved Lebanon. (Samra)

Clearly, a collective narrative was taking shape – one that transcended the prevailing culture of impotence and exclusion. It challenged rigid attitudes that blocked change, while focusing on new ways of seeing. In this unique space, bold views could be analysed in articulation with others as they optimistically moved closer to disrupting and discrediting the dominant Lebanese narrative.

Activism

The assassination of billionaire ex-premier Rafic Hariri on February 14, 2005, followed by a wave of assassinations from 2005–2008 that killed anti-Syrian journalists and politicians, prompted many students to join an active opposition group that called for national unity, while taking a strong stand against Syria and the Syrian-backed Lebanese government. Seeing this as an unprecedented opportunity for mobilisation and activism, students in my workshops became suddenly energised. A widespread youth political culture seemed in the making, one that might alter or at least disrupt the status quo by playing a significant role in instigating broad social and political change. Young people felt empowered to take control of their own destinies and undermine a system starkly defined by sectarianism corruption and stagnation. 'It looks as if our chance to make a difference has finally arrived,' Nadim announced one morning in our workshop. This led to a detailed discussion of the serious ways in which students were becoming deeply involved in the *Intifada*.

Activism has had a long and illustrious history at AUB, particularly in the 1960s and 1970s when, as a cultural and intellectual sanctuary, the University fostered experimentation in ideological doctrines and political platforms away from the reach of oppressive regional regimes. In recent years, however, student generations have lacked such strong political convictions. Rafic Hariri's assassination instantly reversed this pervasive and apathetic trend. In her story, *Painted Reflections*, Hala Alyan (2006) movingly captures the waves of demonstrators demanding regime-change that brought Christians and Muslims together in Martyrs' Square:

> In the next picture a young man, in a sea of demonstrators, is holding up a crucifix in one hand and a Quran in the other. (192)

The Beirut Spring, which succeeded in ending Syria's 30-year hegemony over Lebanon, was largely instigated and sustained by youthful groups, across religious and sectarian divisions, desperate for justice and change:

> The entire country is bristling, a nation that is suddenly wide awake and furious. The stunned, controlled respect and grief that laces the city immediately following Hariri's death seems to have exploded. Scrawled writing appears on the sides of buildings demanding that Syria get out. Groups of young men and women flock to the downtown center near the grave of the political figure now transformed into a reluctant martyr; tents begin to pepper the area. At night cars whiz by with flags flying out, teenage boys stick their upper bodies perilously out of the vehicles as they yell random slogans in Arabic. Demonstrations and counter-demonstrations begin. (Alyan 2006, 192)

In class, earlier obstacles no longer appeared insurmountable. The desire to strip corrupt politicians and many octogenarians of power, eradicate an archaic, dysfunctional political system, instigate a new language of reconciliation, transparency and accountability and address the underlying sources of conflict became powerfully persistent narrative themes:

> The turmoil is due to sectarian divisions and political corruption and it's high time we insist on change through viable, peaceful solutions instead of relying on hate, conflict or unrealistic dreams. (Hani)

Students were quick to distance themselves from the mistakes made by those previously responsible in shaping the country's past:

> Politicians in Lebanon underestimate the swift changes that have occurred. They talk endlessly but in actual fact, they say nothing and think we will listen forever to their empty words. (Amina)

> Those in government must learn to address the concerns of the Lebanese in simple words they can live up to. A new political language is needed. (Raneem)

Sadly, by the end of this period, narrative themes began to drastically shift. The extraordinary enthusiasm initially experienced by student activists was fast dissipating, giving way to disillusioned accounts of what it means to be young and unable to alter a decaying system. A growing demoralising dissonance between expectations and actual lived realities visibly began to erode any hope students once had for change and a brighter future.

Disillusionment

As might be expected, the collective enthusiasm generated by the 2005 uprising did not materialise in any of the progressive transformations so keenly anticipated by youthful groups. The failure of the Independence *Intifada* to achieve national unity between Christians and Muslims, the persistence of sectarian and confessional loyalties in defining the political system and most aspects of life, suddenly left no feasible way forward. Active civil society had been dealt a fatal blow. Consequently, a growing number of my students became legitimately paralysed by the discrepancy between hoped-for-expectations on the one hand, and existing realities on the other. At present, these irreconcilable positions continue to foreground the conversation.

Orhan Pamuk in his 2005 memoir, *Istanbul: Memories of a City*, devotes a chapter to *Hüzün* (melancholy), a mood that casts a shadow of sadness on the cityscape and its inhabitants: 'The black mood shared by millions of people together, the *hüzün* of an entire city' (83).

Not surprisingly, students are now positioning their narratives in a scarred landscape heavy with *hüzün*. The waning of hope and rising tensions create an atmosphere of heavy sadness and melancholy: 'It's absurd to even pretend that change is at all possible. Welcome to the jungle,' Tariq wrote shortly after withdrawing from the Independence *Intifada*. 'I now realize that in no way can our generation alter the power structure.' Mustapha agrees: 'I'm fed up with politics. I don't watch the news or read the papers any more. It's all a waste of time.'

> Suddenly I realized that politicians from all sides, from all sects: Maronites, Orthodox, Catholic, Sunnis, Shiites, Druzes, and God help me if I've missed

any group, acted like the shameless, dishonorable men they are. They lied, they murdered and cheated. But it was us who committed the ultimate crime by holding on to them one more time. We committed a crime against ourselves, against future generations, by disbelieving one another and believing them. (Myrna)

Life here is exhausting. It forces me to re-examine what Lebanon means to me. The future will never be bright. But right now I'm tired, tired of being asked why I refuse to join in the demonstrations, or why I choose not to watch political events on television for 24 hours a day, or even why I look at the sea of Lebanese flags with a vacant, unmoved expression. (Mariana)

Students are adamant when it comes to distancing themselves from politics and the politicians who seem only to perpetuate a corruption-ridden state. With resilient communal loyalties and fractious pluralism on the rise, there is alarm over the escalating language of *retribalisation* and political squabbling that crushes any attempts at a larger political discourse:

Politicians are masterminds at deception and clever words that poison the minds of their blind followers. (Sula)

We are brought up to worship corrupt and inept politicians who only pocket money and remain unaccountable. Honesty is not a virtue in Lebanon. A person is forced to keep quiet, to accept what is corrupt and illegal. (Ali)

Nothing in my country is what it seems. On the surface it's beautiful but in reality it is rotten and ugly. People fight over religion and politics. The Civil War is still alive and well because if issues are solved and the system changes our dirty politicians will be out of work. (Sahar)

I am ashamed to be Lebanese because Lebanon is a country that is built on false hopes and lies. Lebanon is a dead country. (Salah)

Seven years after the Youth *Intifada*, students like Ziad feel betrayed by the politicians who 'simply used us to regain their positions of power'. As revolts and uprisings against authoritarian governments spread across the region, politics in Lebanon is back to the semi-feudal divisions of power and Lebanon's onetime warlords and militia leaders are once again in control. 'The political elite do not address the needs or concerns of the citizens they claim to represent, let alone our generation,' explains Fadia. 'Politics in Lebanon is dirt and anyone who gets involved is corrupt,' insists Hadi. Texts decry the disappearance of youthful idealism and how attempts to redraw and re-imagine a dysfunctional system were made a mockery of:

All our dreams of change are just delusions. Lebanese politicians used us to achieve their own ends. It's true that we accomplished a certain level of national unity after Hariri was killed, but that's it. His assassination was followed by one tragic event after another and now inept politicians are back in office. They have forgotten about their promises to our generation and to the people of Lebanon. What kind of Lebanon is this rotten political class creating for us? Day after day my friends are leaving the country. (Maher)

I hate how all the political parties are at war with one another and all the problems they create. I force myself to stay ignorant. I don't listen to the news and I've stopped reading the papers. (Imad)

While the determination of courageous Arab youth to write their own narratives and challenge ruthless authoritarian regimes has brought a historic transition to a region frozen for generations, my students remain utterly disinterested and disengaged. Nicholas rarely checks the news to see what is happening politically, especially when it's news about the Arab world: 'This is probably the result of my lack of patriotism and disappointment as a Lebanese citizen. I am honestly indifferent about the Arab Spring and feel in no way involved.' Ali shares the same sentiments: 'Whenever I hear about the Arab Spring and the uprisings, I make sure to turn a deaf ear.' Nadia's views are even more telling: 'I don't know what the Arab Spring is and I'm not interested in finding out. It doesn't have any impact on my life.'

Such alarming reactions are undoubtedly linked with the failure of the Beirut Spring. As far as students are concerned, after all the clamour and hope, the change clock in Lebanon never seems to tick past midnight to a new day.

The demoralising dissonance between expectations and existing realities is sadly evident in Mohammad's riveting account of a rude awakening that stifled his youthful optimism:

It was a sunny Sunday morning but I decided not to stay in bed with a cup of coffee while my country stirred with rage. 'Where to, my son?' My father smirked as I wrapped myself in a Lebanese flag, getting ready to free my country. 'Martyrs' Square', I proudly replied as if the future of the nation rested on my shoulders.

A few moments later, I was there shouting at the top of my lungs. From enormous speakers bellowed the familiar voices of politicians who spoke of freedom and justice and independence and all the other 'illusions'. They spoke of the past and of our parents and grandparents who suffered and fought and endured and died for them. They spoke of our Lebanon and every time they paused, I shouted from the top of my lungs until I could no longer breathe. My heart was pounding harder and harder and harder. I painted myself with every color of the Lebanese flag. I became a puppet standing among a million other puppets.

The thought of years and years of war and of my smirking father who had stood in my place a dozen times or more never crossed my mind; nor did the thought of the millions before me who had stood before these very same politicians blindly inhaling their words like the deadly smoke of a comforting cigarette. So I shouted and cheered with all my heart.

By 2:00 pm the crowds started to drift away and I wondered if our cause would drift with them. When I got home my father was drinking a cup of coffee. 'Did you see me there?' I innocently asked. 'How could I? You were no different than the other million out there,' he sarcastically replied. But in his eyes I saw a different answer. Once, he had had the same feeling, believed in the same cause and been willing to fight and die for his country. It's just that he got bored of the deceitful voices of our corrupt politicians and their fathers before them, and, eventually so did I. (Mohammad)

Realistically, of course, my students know they cannot match regional youth uprisings. Even if feudal political affiliations miraculously disappear in Lebanon, religious sentiments are unlikely to dissipate. Jad is keenly aware of the religious divide: 'We had one shining moment during the Beirut Spring when we ignored religion. We all came together to demand a new beginning. But our cunning political elite managed to divide us by awakening religious allegiances.'

Political dynasties have long shaped Lebanese political history, with sons replacing fathers as MPs, ministers and party heads:

Lebanon is a feudal democracy. When a political leader dies he is replaced by his son, daughter, wife, sister, brother, cousin or other family member. (Sabine)

I hate Lebanese politics. I'm sick of all the same predictable surnames! Seriously, we need to get rid of them all. (Abdullah)

I have come to loathe politics. At home, I avoid the living room when my parents are watching the news. I have completely given up hope so why waste time. Politics has failed Lebanon repeatedly. It's the mosquito that won't let you sleep in peace. As much as you try to squash or eliminate it, you always hear the buzz 10 seconds later. Eventually, you just shut your eyes because there is nothing you can do. (Hanan)

Unlike other countries in the region, in Lebanon, Layal points out:

There is not one head of state or one person at the top to target and topple like in Egypt, Syria, Iraq, Libya or Tunisia. Here politicians are like a hydra. Cut off one head and hundreds spring up. Reform would be awesome but it's completely impossible.

Even when it comes to job opportunities, religion, and not qualifications, acts as a filter through which young people are viewed by the government as well as most employers. Bassel complains bitterly about the need for patronage or personal contacts (*wasta*) to secure a job: 'I'm counting the seconds till I leave my country. I want to have equal job opportunities and not depend on *wasta*. I want a profession in a country where I'm rewarded for my hard work.'

> When I graduate I intend to look for a job abroad so my qualifications will count for something. (Adnan)

> It's unfair that my confessional and religious identity determine what job I get. I'll seek employment in a foreign company. (Siham)

Marked by cynicism and detachment, by a clarity and harsher truth, students succumb to the absurd dichotomy of life in a barricaded/hedonistic society; at once a battleground and a playground. Yet the calamity of civil war, the unresolved conflicts and tensions, the darker side of this Janus-like country, are now openly ignored. If there is one aspect that has come to characterise recent behaviour, it's the remarkable way students manage to immunise themselves against internal political conflicts, social ills and regional upheavals. The focus has shifted away from resentment and discontent to the pursuit of happiness and having fun, 'Otherwise,' according to Riad, 'We'll be waiting forever, just like our parents.' As Ghassan Hage, in the Preface to *Lebanon Adrift* (Khalaf 2012), suggests, young Lebanese are 'having fun to forget about the political situation or anything else for that matter: the miserable state of roads and traffic, pollution, chaotic construction, basic social services (rubbish removal, the electricity and water supply).' It's the withdrawal of youth from the social and political to a culture of narcissism and indulgence, a post-ideological, hedonistic life of unrestrained excess that seems only to intensify during periods of extreme uncertainty and danger. For Hasan, the frenzy to experience the good life is largely due to the underlying fear of looming disaster that might strike at any given moment: 'Who knows what kind of violence tomorrow might bring. I was nearly killed during the Israel-Hezbollah 2006 War. Now I want to have as much fun as possible before it's too late.'

Some cope by ignoring disaster when it strikes, even if it's a deadly war:

> The 2006 war with Israel did not affect my lifestyle. We'd go to the Movenpick Hotel. Since it was the main UN base, Israel couldn't attack it. After basking in the sun, we'd shower and go to an Internet café where we'd spend like three or four hours not even thinking about the war. At night we'd watch movies or sit in Starbucks Café. The war was just another summer for me. And it happened to be one of the best. (Talal)

> It was the best summer of my life. Like every summer, I was in Broumana. Honestly, I did not feel there was a war going on. Broumana was buzzing with people. There were fun events and excitement on the streets. Everyone acted like nothing was happening. People partied while the country was being destroyed. (Rawan)

Before themes of defiance began to define narrative texts, students led double lives to avoid inevitable clashes with their parents. Goffman's

(1971) metaphor of frontstage and backstage appropriately exemplified the contradictions they embraced. In *backstage* behaviour, nice personal scripts were relinquished by acting in ways that contradicted the polite moral front they maintained in public or *frontstage* situations. The jarring dissonance that ensued was, according to Reem, 'Damaging to my conscience and sense of wellbeing. It was exhausting to keep juggling and hiding my sexual orientation. Now I am completely open.'

> At the moment, students are no longer willing to 'live a lie'. (Ali)

> A friend of mine was telling me the other day that she leads a double life. She lives in the southern suburbs of Beirut (*al-Dahiya*) and must wear a *abaya* every time she leaves the house. Little does her family know that the second she's out, she turns into a fully-fledged lesbian. It's sad how people must lead two lives in order to satisfy family and community. I refuse to live a life of deceit. I'm constantly clashing with my parents who don't accept that I'm attracted to women. I'm not ashamed of being a lesbian. (Hala)

> When I first started writing my memoir I made sure to put 'I hope' after every paragraph. By the end of the semester, I removed them all and decided to keep only one. I realized it's not constant hoping that moves things forward, it's what I make of my gayness and how I decide I want my life to be. For a very long time I've been trapped in a shell so eager to come out. Now I'm finally out, and, to be honest, I've never been happier. (Suha)

Despite what is happening in Lebanon, or perhaps in spite of it, students are boldly asserting sexual identity openly and in frontstage situations. By pushing sexual boundaries and moving into new, forbidden territory, they are engaging in fluid encounters that sideline and render irrelevant the political change-struggles in the region, let alone the tensions in Lebanon:

> Enjoyment and the appetite for life are instantly gratifying. I go out with my friends every night. We don't think about what is happening in this miserable, failed country. We drink, eat, dance, have fun and sex because we might wake up to violence, war and death tomorrow. (Ahmad)

For Sami, indulging in the delights of physical pleasure provides a welcome escape and puts him in control of his life: 'I will write my own story and not let Lebanon write me.' In his racy narrative, writing becomes a metaphor for the manipulation of sexual desire and control over most aspects of his life:

> I love to write, especially in pencil. I scribble words in the margins or allow them to fall off the page. Writing frames my most severe problems, and packages them. I can read and re-read later. Just like writing, one's sex life should be in pencil. Progressing along effortlessly and happily until one decides to halt, at which point one can continue or go back and erase their steps. In this way, relationships can be easily reversed, one's sex life halted or altered in significant ways.

> I really did care for Aphrodite but she was older than me and had been with more men than the women I have been with. The funny thing is she has probably been with more women than I have too. I owe her everything though. She taught me so much including kinky and unorthodox sex. There were whips and handcuffs, etc. She is extremely beautiful and definitely out of my league. Occasionally, she'd take me to a gay club with her bisexual friends. I would be fed some ecstasy, some shots, then back to the hotel for more sex. She was the most seductive creature I have ever dated. I learned how to combine happiness and pleasure but eventually I couldn't stay with her anymore. The sex became too mundane and it was time to erase the relationship and move on. (Sami)

Riad has freed himself of all constraints, turning to 'the deviant, and insane to the mad, bad, and dangerous', to escape a society and political system 'beyond repair':

> After frequenting scandalous locations around Lebanon, I finally found myself within a social circle of transvestite prostitutes whose world was the polar opposite of anything I was used to. Together we went through dangerous adventures. This fascinated me immensely and fueled the writing of my short story *Alex of Berytus*. The story revolves around Alex, a runaway homosexual who sells his body to Gulf men in order to live. The details are partially made-up, but also drawn from the experiences I lived. I actually did befriend a transvestite prostitute by the name of Alex who I 'might have' had living with me in the AUB dorms, illegally, in the spring of 2009. The close contact with his world, though scandalous, was fruitful and beneficial.

Mahdavi (2011) insightfully shows how young people view changes in sexuality and social behaviour as a way of de-legitimising and de-stabilising the power of a regime claiming to have brought moral values:

> Perhaps there is nowhere in the world where the stakes of having fun are higher than in present day Iran. Young people from all socioeconomic backgrounds are increasingly seeking to carve out recreational spaces for themselves against the backdrop of a repressive regime. (149)

The formation of fun spaces is a welcome exit from a public/political arena that has manipulated and made a mockery of youthful views seeking change. It's an attempt to 'other' those who have so callously 'othered' and excluded them. By asserting agency in spheres they can control, students have created an alternative paradigm of youth culture that is unthreatening and, as a result, ignored by those in power. 'As long as we don't challenge anything political or religious we can do whatever we like,' Samia explains, 'Our families sometimes try to interfere in our private lives but they can't stop us from having all the fun, sex and plastic surgery we want.'

As Samir Khalaf argues in *Lebanon Adrift* (2012), the Lebanese have lost their moorings, direction and sense of control. There is a shift away from the social and political to a life of shallowness, consumerism and pleasure. This provides 'a sense of immunity from a traumatizing environment' (Hage 2012, in Preface to Khalaf 2012, 8).

Billboards across the country advertise easily obtainable bank loans for plastic surgery. Rarely does a semester pass without four or five women students appearing in class with nose bandages. When the bandages are removed, their noses are usually identical. During one workshop session, when the conversation turned to the preoccupation with body image, Hadi said, 'There are new and "in" nose shapes every season. You know the year surgery is performed by the shape of the nose.' Manal expressed her pride at having undergone nose surgery twice because she 'hated the result the first time'. She's 'delighted to be young at a time when I can transform any part of my body that I don't like because beautiful women get what they want in life'.

Despite indulging in the good life, my students remain keenly aware of limited professional opportunities, a high cost of living and a deteriorating security situation. Recent statistics show that the exodus of young Lebanese college graduates has reached dramatic proportions.

During a discussion in the spring semester of 2012, I vividly recall how many of my bright students had already decided to join the Lebanese diaspora:

> My only hope for a decent future is to get as far away as possible from this oppressive country. (Dima)

> I, too, have lost all hope and am counting the days till I leave. (Ahmad)

> Lebanon is bubbly and beautiful but unstable and dangerous. I'm definitely leaving. (Farouq)

Anthony had developed a clever strategy. He's:

> Careful not to get attached. Distance and indifference on my part will make leaving easier. I've trained myself to let go of everything and everyone, even girls. My plan has been successful and now I can emigrate with no emotional ties or pain. Lebanon gives nothing to its citizens, even to the best. Instead, it injects us with daily stress.

> Graduation is upon me and I can't wait to leave this country I've lost hope in. (Amer)

> Our country is built on hatred, mistrust and corruption. People here do not accept difference. They are intolerant, violent and heavily armed. Conflict is inevitable. I'm not staying around to witness more death and destruction. (Rashid)

While orchestrating exit strategies, students continue to fiercely contest the denial tactics of older generations as well as their resilience and endless patience:

> My generation is leaving because we are disgusted with everything, especially pressure from our families to be patient and resilient. Right now, my solution is to have a good time until I can leave. (Yusif)

> As young Lebanese we are brought up to be patient about things that we know will never happen. We're conditioned to become desensitized and blasé. What most societies take for granted, we're still patiently waiting for. So we live with power and water shortages, threats of sectarian violence from militia groups, political and other forms of corruption, a confessional system, mad, unplanned construction, rotting infrastructure and the knowledge that history will continue to repeat itself. I'm not religious. I do not believe in Allah but if He truly does exist, then I can say with human certainty that he has forsaken this country a long time ago. (Leila)

Some closing thoughts

In most societies, the insecurities of young people are associated with the inevitable process of becoming an adult, particularly in post-modern settings where fluidity and uncertainty have replaced structure and tradition. For young Lebanese, roughly half the population, these tensions are hugely compounded. As traditional vectors of stability and loyalty (family and state) are being rejected, employment, security and public discourse remain absent. Within this void, the youth are trapped in a poignant, unsettling predicament. Ironically, they are celebrated as the 'hope of the future', yet deprived of a unified history, stable political system and employment opportunities. Worse still, their voices are silenced or marginalised at a time when Lebanon's historical legacy of unresolved conflict is desperately in need of innovative ways to move beyond a turbulent post-war era.

Within this context, narratives are hugely significant. They matter because they reveal what is and what could and should be. We are conditioned to 'expect' stories with a particular structure, with protagonists and villains, good and bad forces, battles to be fought and obstacles to overcome. Clearly, over the years, my students have abandoned such plots. Rife with a total negativity, disillusioned and defiant, they are busy creating pleasurable, even promiscuous spaces for narcissistic excess. Tragically, in this country of alarming contradictions, simultaneously a battleground and playground, playground activities have prevailed. The political activism, youth-led rebellions and change-struggles resulting from Hariri's assassination in 2005 succeeded, only briefly, in sparking optimistic themes of transformation that demanded an end to the decades-long political strife and altering a rigid, intolerant landscape.

Sadly, a glaring discrepancy between earlier expectations and today's harsh realities is currently defining the conversation, fuelling a mood of lethargy and indifference. Bitterness abounds concerning existing archaic institutions, corrupt, inept politicians and their refusal to address crucial issues. Obstacles to change are seen as insurmountable and, consequently, not worth fighting for. With enthusiasm dissipating, even ongoing regional uprisings seem only to strengthen youth apathy and post-ideological stances. Students, many of whom have the capacity to be effective problem solvers and change makers, are rejecting all forms of public discourse and civic engagement.

In such an anachronistic post-war setting, where sectarian tensions remain high in the wake of regional wars and conflicts, students are no longer interested in reclaiming an open, pluralistic environment conducive to a modicum of tolerance and coexistence. As they indulge in the trappings of a hedonistic culture, negotiable spaces are inevitably shrinking. Continuing the conversation of how and where to find enabling venues for youth citizenship, alongside new ways of articulating it, remains problematic. Genuine confusion abounds regarding how to re-energise students who lack serious concern and conviction, particularly given the legacy of exclusion, fear and mistrust in the country. What enabling venues, modes of solidarity, new concepts and discourse can be developed to reverse the absent nature of youth participation when past attempts to move beyond dysfunctional traditional and institutional frameworks and paradoxes have failed?

Admittedly, the decision of young people to withdraw from active citizenship will define the conversation for years to come, particularly given the absence of compelling new, non-confrontational views. Yet, narrative engagement, in a modest way, continues to open up enabling spaces in an atmosphere of growing intolerance and latent hostility. Making silenced voices heard remains crucial to a country in dire need of reconciliation and change. Through meaningful text creation students from diverse backgrounds challenge strictures imposed by exclusionary mindsets and replace them with innovative ways of seeing. As regional sectarian divisions fuel local sectarian rivalries, the need to re-engage citizen consciousness among educated young Lebanese is vital. Rekindling youthful participation can play a significant role in disrupting a dangerous sectarian narrative that is fast threatening to entangle Lebanon in yet another brutal war.

Acknowledgements

This publication was made possible in part by a grant from the Issam Fares Institute for Public Policy and International Affairs at the American University of Beirut as part of the 'Youth in the Arab World Program'.

References

Alyan, Hala. 2006. "Painted Reflections." In *Hikayat: Short Stories by Lebanese Women*, edited by Roseanne Khalaf, 192–201. London: Saqi.

Asseily, Alexandra. 2009. "Exploring Stories to Find the Storyteller." In *Exploring Selfhood: Finding Ourselves, Finding Our Stories in Life Narratives*, edited by S. Gill and I. Goodson, 37–49. Brighton: Guerrand-Hermes Foundation.

Bauman, Zygmunt. 2000. *Liquid Modernity*. Oxford: Blackwell.

Bloom, Leslie. 1996. "Stories of One's Own: Nonunitary Subjectivity in Narrative Representation." *Qualitative Inquiry* 2 (2): 176–197.

Boym, Sveltana. 1996. "Estrangement as a Life Style." In *Exile and Creativity: Signposts, Travelers, Outsiders, Backward Glances*. edited by Susan Rubin Suleiman, 241–262. Durham, NC: Duke University Press.

Charmaz, Kathy, and Richard Mitchell. 1997. "The Myth of Silent Authorship: Self, Substance and Style in Ethnographic Writing." In *Reflexivity and Voice*, edited by Rosanna Hertz, 193–215. London: Sage.

Ewick, Patricia, and Susan Silbey. 1995. "Subversive Stories and Hegemonic Tales: Towards a Sociology of Narrative." *Law and Society Review* 29 (2): 197–226.

Gahre, Christian. 2011. "Youth Networks, Space and Political Mobilization: Lebanon's Independence *Intifada*." In *Arab Youth: Social Mobilization in Times of Risk*, edited by Samir Khalaf and Roseanne Khalaf, 277–300. London: Saqi.

Giddens, Anthony. 1991. *Modernity and Self-Identity: Self and Society in the Late Modern Age*. Cambridge: Polity Press.

Gill, Scherto, ed. 2009. *Introduction to Exploring Selfhood: Finding Ourselves, Finding Our Stories in Life Narratives*. Brighton: Guerrand-Hermes Foundation.

Goffman, Erving. 1971. *The Presentation of Self in Everyday Life*. New York, NY: Doubleday.

Goodson, Ivor. 2009. "Looking at the Big Picture 'Selfhood in Context': Exploring Cultural Geographies of Selfhood." In *Exploring Selfhood: Finding Ourselves, Finding Our Stories in Life Narratives*, edited by Scherto Gill, 33–35. Brighton: Guerrand-Hermès Foundation.

Goodson, Ivor, and Scherto Gill. Forthcoming 2014. *Narrative Learning and Critical Pedagogy*. London: Bloomsbury.

Hage, Ghassan. 2012. "Preface." In *Lebanon Adrift: From Battleground to Playground*, by Samir Khalaf. London: Saqi.

Halasa, Malu, and Roseanne Khalaf, eds. 2004. *Transit Beirut: New Writing and Images*. London: Saqi.

Hirsh, Marianne. 1997. *Family Frames: Photography, Narrative and Postmemory*. Cambridge, MA: Harvard University Press.

Hirsh, Marianne. 1998. "Past Lives: Postmemories in Exile." In *Exile and Creativity: Signposts, Travelers, Outsiders, Backward Glances*, edited by Susan Rubin Suleiman, 418–446. Durham, NC: Duke University Press.

Kamler, Barbara. 2001. *Relocating the Personal*. New York, NY: State University of New York Press.

Kegels, Nicolien. 2011. "In Good Times or Bad? Discourse on the Identity of Lebanese Upper Class Youth." In *Arab Youth: Social Mobilization in Times of Risk*, edited by Samir Khalaf and Roseanne Khalaf, 176–193. London: Saqi.

Khalaf, Roseanne. 2009. "Youthful Voices in Post-War Lebanon." *Journal of Middle Eastern Studies* 63 (1): 49–68.

Khalaf, Samir. 2012. *Lebanon Adrift*. London: Saqi.

Khalaf, Samir, and Roseanne Khalaf, eds. 2011. *Arab Youth: Social Mobilization in Times of Risk*. London: Saqi.

Larkin, Craig. 2011. "Between Silences and Screams: The Lebanese Postmemory Experience." In *Arab Youth: Social Mobilization in Times of Risk*, edited by Samir Khalaf and Roseanne Khalaf, 127–145. London: Saqi.

Mahdavi, Pardis. 2011. "The Politics of Fun in the Islamic Republic of Iran: Re-Creation and Recreation." In *Arab Youth: Social Mobilization in Times of Risk*, edited by Samir Khalaf and Roseanne Khalaf, 149–175. London: Saqi.

Pamuk, Orhan. 2005. *Istanbul: Memories of a City*. London: Faber & Faber.

Pinar, William. 1997. "Regimes of Reason and the Male Narrative Voice." In *Representation and the Text*, edited by W. Tierney and Y. Lincoln, 81–113. Albany: State University of New York Press.

Said, Edward. 1991. "Identity, Authority and Freedom: The Potentate and the Traveler." *Transition* 21 (54): 4–18.

Scarry, Elaine. 1985. *The Body in Pain*. Oxford: Oxford University Press.

Reconciliation through dialogical nostalgia in post-conflict societies: a curriculum to intersect

Petro du Preez

Edu-HRight Unit, Faculty of Education Sciences, North-West University, Potchefstroom, South Africa

> The curriculum has been proposed as a powerful means with the potential to initiate social transformation. It reflects the dominant social, economical and political discourses and for this reason it seems reasonable to situate reconciliatory discourses in relation to the curriculum. Whilst curriculum scholars mostly agree that we need to seek new directions and ways of understanding curriculum, there is little consensus about the direction the field should take. Two particular issues that this article addresses are the tendency of curriculum practitioners to tackle social issues at a symptomatic level instead of considering the roots of the problems, and the over-emphasis on the political dimension with little or no attention given to the ethical dimensions of the curriculum. In an attempt to develop new ways of understanding curriculum and enabling social change, I explore nostalgia as a way to stimulate dialogue over competing narratives. To facilitate this exploration, I draw on the notion of the ethical turn in the study of curriculum and the theory of intersectionality. Examples from South Africa are used to develop the argument. I conclude by situating the discussion in the context of other post-conflict societies where reconciliation is needed.

Narratives of difference

Two decades after the abolition of apartheid in South Africa, racial segregation and violence still feature prominently in the verbal and symbolic encounters between people of diverse descent. Lived experiences and social realities are expressed in very different, typified narratives.[1] These typified narratives are made up of a variety of symbols, myths and dialects – each representing a cluster of voices or dominant discourses. At times, it is difficult for people to converse beyond their own narratives or even dominant, typified narratives. In the words of Slattery (2006), at times, it seems impossible to deal with the 'shifting vantage points among various stakeholders' and to arrive at 'the intersections of competing voices' (282). In his book, *We Need to Talk*, Jonathan Jansen (2011) explores ways that will lead South Africans to the intersections of their competing, typified narratives, thus making reconciliation possible. The examples from his work and those of others are used in this article to illustrate how different forms of nostalgia underpin competing narratives and how these forms of nostalgia often prevent the intersection of competing narratives. Furthermore, the purpose of these examples is to corroborate theoretical arguments, rather than to provide concrete empirical evidence (cf. Margalit 2002).

Considering the need to arrive at the intersection of competing narratives I will proceed by developing my main argument: reconceptualising nostalgia in an artful manner makes it possible to begin conceptualising the space where competing narratives could intersect. To facilitate the development of this argument, the following question is asked: How can we rethink nostalgia to open pathways for dialogue that can lead us to the intersections of competing narratives? In what follows, I will develop the notion of nostalgia as a starting point for conceptualising the space where competing narratives could intersect through dialogue. Thereafter, I will explore what this argument might mean for curriculum theorising through asking: In what ways can the theory of curriculum be conceptualised to accommodate dialogical nostalgia? I hope that this article will conceptually contribute to curriculum theorising that could facilitate reconciliatory processes in post-conflict societies like South Africa through interactive, reflective and action-driven dialogue. In this theoretical pursuit, the significance of the ethical turn in the study of curriculum is explored in conjunction with the notion of intersectionality. Curriculum in this article will not refer to the curriculum as merely a syllabus, but 'as a complicated conversation among teachers and students focused on texts and the concepts they communicate in specific places at particular historical moments' (Pinar 2010, 177).

The following topics will be addressed and endorsed by several examples: an exploration of the notion of nostalgia and its various embodiments, an exploration of the significance of the ethical turn in curriculum, and a conceptualisation of reflective, dialogical nostalgia in the context of a curriculum to intersect.

Exploring nostalgia

The exploration of the notion of nostalgia that follows will include: an etymological and genealogical clarification, a discussion on the elements constituting nostalgia, the levels of irony embedded in nostalgia, the links between history, memory and nostalgia, and two different forms of nostalgia. In essence, it will be argued that nostalgia is an ethical imperative, one that concerns the past, present and future. In addition, nostalgia will be positioned as a multifaceted entity that concerns social change in as far as it is conceptualised as dialogical, i.e., interactive, reflective and action-orientated.

From doctors to poets and philosophers

The Greek etymological roots of the concept nostalgia are *nostos* (home or space) and *algia* (longing for another time). Nostalgia was first introduced as a medical and pathological condition in 1688 by the Swiss physician Johannes Hofer (Davis 1979). It was commonly associated with conditions such as melancholy and obsessive compulsive behaviour (Davis 1979). The concept was gradually demedicalised and depsychologised in the 1950s, when it was assimilated in popular speech in the USA (Davis 1979). It commonly became associated with a sentimental recall of emotions such as love, jealousy and fear in a passive, soothing fashion (Davis 1979). This understanding of nostalgia moved the responsibility for its exploration from doctors to poets and philosophers (Boym 2001).[2]

Before engaging in a more multifaceted exploration of nostalgia, it is important to take note of five seminal works of the last century that have shaped our evolving understanding of nostalgia, at least from a Western perspective. The first of these, *Nostalgia: An Existential Exploration of Longing and Fulfilment in the Modern Age*, was written by Ralph Harper in 1966. An earlier version of this was published as *The Sleeping Beauty* (1955). The 1966 edition could be roughly described as a philosophical meditation or aesthetic contemplation of nostalgia in relation to the notions of presence and fulfilment in the context of poetic justice. The second of these seminal works was written by Fred Davis in 1979 and entitled *Yearning for Yesterday: A Sociology of Nostalgia*. In this sociology, Davis aims to create an understanding of the general conditions and circumstances that evoke nostalgic feelings and examine some of these through phenomenological interviews. The third work on nostalgia is *The Future of Nostalgia*, which was written by Svetlana Boym in 2001. Boym politicises nostalgia in an attempt to reveal its many facets and inherent complexity. In doing so, she elevates the discourse of nostalgia from what is merely sentimental and pacifying discourse to a highly politicised and ethical phenomenon. This is done mainly by distinguishing between restorative and reflective nostalgia. These notions will be explored in the remainder of this article. The fourth work that has contributed to the evolution of nostalgia, *Native Nostalgia*, emanated from the pen of Jacob Dlamini in 2010. For the most part, Dlamini's reflective nostalgic narrative about his political memory of childhood in apartheid South Africa takes a similar line to Boym. Also drawing on the work of Boym, is Dennis Walder (2010) in his book *Postcolonial Nostalgias: Writing, Representation, and Memory*. In this book he argues that the nature of nostalgia should be understood in its various embodiments because it has the potential to (re)connect the individual with the past and with communities. In addition, he argues that nostalgia provides us with an ethical imperative to recognise the demand of the other, whereby I would add the recognition of the same. The lack of rigorous scrutiny of the commodification of particular memories and histories in popular media as a result of postmodernism could also effectively be facilitated when the theory of nostalgia is applied (Walder 2010).

All five books refer explicitly to space and time – the central elements that constitute nostalgia and that have the potential to assist us in reconceptualising the idea. What is also noticeable is how the discourse of nostalgia has moved from *nostalgia as sentiment* toward *nostalgia as politics*. In this regard, Boym (2001) postulates that '[w]hen nostalgia turns political, romance is connected to nation building and native songs are purified. The official memory of the nation-state does not tolerate useless nostalgia, nostalgia for its own sake' (14). For the purpose of this article, I will focus mostly on Boym (2001), Dlamini (2010) and Walder (2010), who politicise nostalgia, since these (as will be indicated below) better represent the complexity of nostalgia and have more obvious applications to curriculum, which is inherently political in nature.

Irony through space and time

Despite its changing etymological nature, nostalgia is still conceptualised in terms of a largely linear, one-dimensional understanding of time and a one-dimensional understanding of space. Here, time as an element of nostalgia is viewed as *chronos* (Gk.), which implies a sequential, quantitative understanding of time, and the space element of nostalgia is understood as *chõros* (Gk.), which refers to any space within the parameters of a border (a physical home in the literal sense of the word). However, later descriptions of nostalgia recognise the complex nature of nostalgia, especially the way time, space and movement coincide or intersect (Dlamini 2010). Dlamini asserts that:

> ... nostalgia, 'a sentiment of loss and displacement', is an incurable condition of modernity. ... the irony about nostalgia is that, for all its fixation with the past, it is essentially about the present. It is about present anxieties refracted through the prism of the past. ... it is usually when people feel themselves adrift in a world seemingly out of control that they come down with nostalgia. (16)

From this it is clear that nostalgia consists of a dynamic interplay of emotion (anxiety), time (past, present, future), space (a place or home in the literal and figurative sense) and movement (in time and space) – a nexus of dimensions resulting in the complexity of nostalgia. In this sense, the notion of time cannot be based on *chronos*, but needs to be extended to *kairos*

(Gk.). *Kairos* does not refer to sequential time counted in hours, minutes and seconds that tends to compartmentalise and schedule human existence (Slattery 2006). Rather, *kairos* (Gk.) denotes a supreme moment, the birth of a new era, and is qualitative in nature. Similarly, space cannot be limited to *chõros*, but needs to be understood as *kenón* (Gk.) and *cháos* (Gk.), terms that refer to infinite space characterised by randomness and complex disorder.

The notions of time and space and the inherent movement they suggest give rise to two levels of irony in nostalgia. The first of these emanates from the element of time in nostalgia. This suggests that nostalgia is not only about the past (as Dlamini rightly suggests) but is also simultaneously about the present and the future. An understanding of time as *kairos* is described by scholars as follows:

> 'what happened once upon a time happens all the time' [Abraham Joshua Heshel], 'there is no such thing as the past because the past is still present' [William Faulkner], 'the present holds within itself the complete sum of existence, backwards and forwards, that whole amplitude of time which is eternity' [Alfred North Whitehead] and 'the true present is nothing else but the eternity that is immanent in time' [Jürgen Moltmann]. (Slattery 2006, 85)

In effect, this conception explains why one could be nostalgic about the future. This level of nostalgia is important since it inevitably suggests that *kairos* time and *kenón* and *cháos* space make an understanding of nostalgia possible that surpasses its absolute and static roots. This journey of understanding is embedded in multidimensional change.

The first layer of irony also leads to the second layer, which is captured in the ability of nostalgia to facilitate social change as opposed to stagnation. McLeod and Thomson (2009) explain that:

> ... in times of rapid change we tend to assuage 'apprehension of the future by retrieving the worth of the past' ... and that this 'allows time for needed change to be assimilated while giving the appearance ... of meaningful links to the past'. (8)

Jedlowski (as quoted in McLeod and Thomson 2009) supplements this:

> ... the past structures the present through its legacy, but it is the present that selects this legacy, preserving some aspects or forgetting others, and which constantly reformulates our image of this past by repeatedly recounting the story. (15)

The two levels of irony in nostalgia could be summarised as follows: (1) although it seems to be about the past, it is about the intersection of the past, present and future; and (2) although it hints toward stagnation in traditional understandings of the word, it is essentially about social change.

These levels of irony are important in that they enable us to distinguish between different forms of nostalgia. Following up on Walder's (2010) suggestion that varieties of nostalgia are worth pursuing, two of these varieties or forms will be discussed after the link between nostalgia, memory and history has been alluded to.

In the twilight zone between memory and history

Venturing into the field of nostalgia necessitates an exploration into its conceptual connection to theories of (collective) memory and history. For Walder (2010), nostalgia as theory penetrates the twilight zone between memory and history. Margalit (2002) argues that memory is often perceived as a common sense, emotional notion linked to myth and enchanted ideas, whereas history is more often connected with the (objective) 'truth' – the disenchanted ideas of the past – that warrants the label of science. In similar vein to Boym (2001), Margalit (2002) criticises an understanding of nostalgia that is confined to sentimentality.

Both Walder (2010) and Margalit (2002) perceive of nostalgia as intertwined with memory. For Walder (2010) nostalgia can begin with desire (or enchanted ideas) but could also potentially lead to truth (or disenchanted history). Margalit (2002) postulates that nostalgia is an aspect of shared memory. Shared memory, unlike common memory, is not a mere combination of first-hand memory of people remembering a particular episode: it includes dialogue about deferred experience that calibrates different views or perspectives regarding common memory (Margalit 2002).

For Walder (2010), nostalgia is a complex form of representation of the past: one that is both pervasive and a source of understanding and creativity. He argues that amidst the culture of 'memory fatigue' in especially literary and cultural studies, nostalgia as a body of scholarship has received very little attention (Walder 2010, 4).

Next, I will argue that we need to free nostalgia from the chains of sentiment, stagnation and the one-dimensionality of truth. To do this we need to expand our understanding of nostalgia's core elements – space and time. In the act of unchaining the core elements of nostalgia, we are able to set it free from its etymological foundation – longing for a home – to enable new ways of understanding. This might enable us to reconceptualise nostalgia as a progressive phenomenon with the potential to facilitate unity in difference and difference for unity through dialogue.

Silent and dialogical nostalgia

Boym's (2001) distinction between restorative and reflective nostalgia is helpful in developing the concept of nostalgia. In what follows, I will discuss her ideas on restorative and reflective nostalgia and illustrate how restorative nostalgia can be applied to the South African context by means of several examples. I will use the work of Dlamini (2010) to illustrate the effect of reflective nostalgia. It should be noted that these two forms of nostalgia are not binary opposites – in reality they often overlap.

For Boym (2001, xvii) restorative nostalgia is essentially about the restoration of origins and the inherent conspiracy in the act of restoration. The former could be described in terms of Booth's (1999) understanding of traditionalism and the latter in terms of culturalism. Culturalism denotes the act of preserving culture in traditionalist terms for the purpose of safeguarding conservative power interests (Booth 1999). The notion of preserving culture through traditionalism denotes the act of reconstructing a lost home; thus the focus is on what divides us – home or *nostos* (culture) – and not on what we share, that is, the feeling of longing or *algia* (Boym 2001). In safeguarding the interests of conservative power, the restorative nostalgic protects absolute truths embedded in traditional terms by using culturalist symbols retrieved from memory, even though these symbols are often misinterpreted (Boym 2001). Restorative nostalgia relies on time as a one-directional, linear notion and space as a one-dimensional entity with clear boundaries. This conceptualisation leads to the absolutisation of the difference between the past, present and future as isolated entities. Boym (2001) states that for the restorative nostalgic, the past '… is a value for the present; the past is not a duration but a perfect snapshot' (49). Next, I will turn to two typified narratives to illustrate how restorative nostalgia works, how it is often institutionalised (both overtly and tacitly) and how it creates divisions amongst people.

Two decades after the abolition of apartheid in South Africa, many instances of hate speech and racism are still being documented, highlighting the discrepancy between typified narratives. In one instance, four white Afrikaans-speaking students humiliated black cleaning staff during a university residence mock initiation ritual. This initiation ritual was orchestrated by the four male students in protest against the hostel integration policy (that made racial integration in hostels compulsory) first introduced by the university in June 2007 (Marais and De Wet 2009). During this initiation ritual, the black cleaning staff had to compete in a beer-drinking contest, a footrace and a dancing activity and then consume food that had seemingly been urinated on (Fairbanks 2010; Soudien 2010). This videotaped incident apparently occurred in September 2007 (Marais and De Wet 2009) and was published online in February 2008 (Fairbanks 2010). The purpose of the video was to provocatively demonstrate a process of finding a suitable black subject to join the residence (Soudien 2010). Referred to as the Reitz event, this incident reveals the difference and discrimination still embedded in the rainbow nation and the symbolic ways in which racism still surfaces, thus reducing the prospect of unity. In the words of Fairbanks (2010), 'The video seemed like a flare-up indicating a deeper national disease' (15). The matter was taken up by the Equality Court, the four students were found guilty on charges of *crimen injuria* and fined an amount of R20,000 each (Soudien 2010). Whether this sentence was appropriate and whether justice has been done is disputable and beyond the scope of this article, what is important is the question asked by Soudien (2010): Did anyone ever ask the students what they were thinking when they constructed the scene? The Reitz event, which is an attempt to restore tradition to manage continuity with the past, demonstrates how a ritual of symbolic nature is used to inculcate certain traditionalist values and norms in opposition to change (Boym 2001). Tradition in this sense refers to the apartheid era in which white males enjoyed higher status and power than non-whites and females. The Reitz event clearly demonstrates how tradition is not so much restored as reinvented. This event could also be translated as an act of rebuilding *nostos* through reliving an ideology of white supremacy and in so doing forfeiting critical thinking for emotional bonding (Boym 2001).

In a second instance, the former leader of the Youth League of the African National Congress (the leading political party in South Africa), Julius Malema[3] (born on 3 March 1981), could be described as a popular and charismatic but controversial leader. One author states that Malema's, '... reckless and disrespectful pronouncements under the guise of militancy were taken as gospel by his admirers' (Commey 2011b, 74). Malema, at the aged of nine, joined the nationalist youth movement – Masupatsela – that had the purpose of removing all apartheid posters and propaganda (Commey 2011a). In addition to his 'forceful style' and use of 'populist themes' that are often racialised (Commey 2011b, 74), he is notorious for his use of hate speech. One instance of this occurred during an interview with a BBC journalist and the other when he sang the chorus 'Dubul' iBhunu' (kill the 'boer' [farmer] – referring to white Afrikaans-speaking people) of the song 'Ayasab' amagwala' (the cowards are scared) during a rally on a university campus. Fairbanks (2010), too, criticises Malema's '... cryptic sayings – "Don't come here with that white tendency", "This is not America, it's Africa", "Go out, you bloody agent"' (15). Apart from being racist, these verbal and symbolic narratives demonstrate an overt feeling of nostalgia, or longing for a(n) (idealistic) past, a past characterised by the struggle against apartheid. One might ask why a young man like Malema, who was only a young child when apartheid was abolished (see Jansen 2009), makes such controversial and radical utterances. The answer may lie in another view of the past. Boym (2001) states that restorative nostalgia is characterised by the following reasoning: '"They" conspire against "our" homecoming, hence "we" have to conspire against "them" in order to restore "our" imagined community' (43). An example of this reasoning is to be found in two of Malema's Twitter tweets. He stated that, '[w]hites had a head-start in the "race" and therefore they carry almost a century's advantage in everything in SA [South Africa]' (August 11, 2011) and, '[t]he race issue is not just the colour of one's skin but the race we run as blacks to catch up' (August 11, 2011). The problem with this reasoning is that it artificially divides black ('we') and white ('them') by oversimplifying history. In this regard, Jansen (2011) states, '… as long as the historical narrative retains "good black victims" and "bad white perpetrators", we don't stand a chance of reconstructing and reconciling in the beloved country' (8).

Jansen (2011) recalls the meeting that he had with Julius Malema about the Reitz event in his office at the University of the Free State, where the event occurred. Against the background of protesters singing and chanting outside ('a potentially explosive event'), Malema asked Jansen why he decided 'to *forgive* institutional charges against the Reitz four' (Jansen 2011, 21, emphasis added). Jansen then described how he spent 40 minutes justifying this act of forgiveness and how the expression on Malema's face changed from one of condemnation to one of appreciation and understanding. This meeting illustrates the power of artful reconceptualisation of the intersection of competing narratives.

Whereas restorative nostalgia focuses on what divides us, reflective nostalgia focuses on what we share: longing or *algia*. It is this characteristic that creates the paradoxical nature of nostalgia (Boym 2001) and that, I would argue, creates the potential for nostalgia to unite us through respect for and understanding of difference. The meditative undertone of reflective nostalgia delays homecoming by disrupting absolute truths. Boym (2001) argues that, '[r]eflective nostalgia does not follow a single plot but explores ways of inhabiting many places at once and imagining different time zones; it loves details, not symbols' (xviii). In this, we also see that reflective nostalgia imagines time and space as complex, detailed entities not to be reduced to linear, boundaried entities. Nostalgia is both an ethical and a creative challenge, which 'take[s] sensual delight in the texture of time not measurable by clocks and calendars' (Boym 2001, 49).

The ethical and creative challenge of reflective nostalgia is demonstrated in Dlamini's (2010) individual narrative. Instead of 'reconstructing emblems and rituals of home … to conquer and spatialize time', he 'cherishes shattered fragments of memory and temporalizes space' in 'ironic and humorous' ways (Boym 2001, 49). Most importantly, his narrative demonstrates critical thinking about the crucial relationship between the past, present and future and the inability to reinvent a home (Boym 2001). He explores this crucial relationship by playing with the different levels of irony in nostalgia.

An example of how Dlamini (2010) ironically challenges linear conceptions of time, one-dimensional conceptions of space and inert movement is captured in the following quote:

> … people's lives have changed. … It is all too often taken for granted that the story of black South Africa is one long romance, starting in some golden age during which Africans lived in harmony with the land and each other,

followed by the trials and tribulations of European conquest, segregation and apartheid, and ending in triumph with Nelson Mandela. ... In this romantic telling, there is a neat separation between a merry precolonial Africa, a miserable apartheid South Africa and a marvellous new South Africa in which everyone is living democratically ever after. That, alas, is not so. There are many South Africans for whom the past, the present and the future are not discrete wholes, with clear splits between them. (12)

In this quote, we see how the linear sentiment underpinning nostalgia is disrupted and the complex intersection of time and politics underscored. Dlamini (2010) manages to show how the 'symbols of the past' (in a restorative conception of nostalgia) could be reconstructed as a detailed reflection that enables us to observe moments of complex intersection. There are two interesting examples that demonstrate this intersection. Firstly, Dlamini describes how the radio – in a restorative conception – could be described as a symbol of apartheid in that it served as the propaganda tool of the apartheid government. However, in reflecting on this, he explained how the radio had an opposite effect on him, because it awakened political consciousness in him and led him to pursue political journalism as a career. Secondly, he dedicates a chapter to the topic: 'The Language of Nostalgia' (135–163). This chapter deals with Afrikaans, the symbolic language of apartheid and the oppressor. He describes how this language filtered into the dialect of other African languages and how adults in rural areas used to speak Afrikaans when they didn't want children to understand what they were speaking about. The point is that instead of demonising the symbol of Afrikaans, Dlamini nostalgically reflects upon it and reveals the many layers of meaning attached to such symbols. In doing so, he leads us to an understanding of intersecting intricacies in society, which open pathways for dialoguing difference in understanding in an attempt to reconcile difference.

What is clear from Dlamini's (2010) explorations is that he focuses on what we share. He troubles absolute truths through revealing the different understandings that underpin a symbol. In doing so, he transcends the sentiment that often demarcates people's understanding of nostalgia and politicises the nature of nostalgia as a multifaceted entity. What he also manages to do is to unveil the silence of nostalgia and use it as a dialogical mechanism to unearth complexity, making it possible for nostalgia to lead us to the intersections of competing narratives. It is within this context that I prefer using the terms 'silenced nostalgia' and 'dialogical nostalgia'. The latter refers to dialogue, stimulated by nostalgia, that is interactive, reflective and action-orientated.

Embracing the ethical turn in curriculum through intersectionality

Traditional conceptions of curriculum (i.e., traditionalism, conceptual-empiricism and reconceptualism) (see Pinar 2009) cannot address questions such as whether or how a curriculum can help to create a more peaceful society or where the ethic of diversity within unity and social cohesion are valued. This is so because, in these conceptions, curriculum is mostly perceived from an instrumentalist or political approach and pays little heed to the ethical dimension of the curriculum. As Morrison (2004) suggests:

> Recycling ideas leads to curriculum closure; it goes nowhere. Novelty and originality are required to move forward the fields of curriculum theory and development. However one may wish to package it, the message is the same: move on; discover and invent new worlds and new ideas. (487)

Cary (2007) emphasises that research into curriculum spaces should reflect an ethical turn since this will enable us to rethink and act upon the strategic language we use to express *'the way we know what we know'* (134–135, emphasis in original). For Pinar (2010, 178) the process of rethinking and acting curriculum also includes research about individual engagements with multiple narratives in realising civic ideals. The ethical turn in philosophy is a counter movement in postmodernist philosophy that expresses a concern with the debunking of ethics. The ethical turn also stresses aesthetic expression in relation to ethics. Applied to curriculum, the ethical turn focuses on the debunking of ethics in education and aims to put the spotlight on ethics in curriculum discourses in an attempt to address questions of (amongst other things) competing narratives (Cary 2007; Pinar 2011).

Badiou (2002), in assessing the validity of the ethical turn (Gillespie 2001), criticises the current state of ethical affairs as an ethical ideology stemming from liberal-humanism. He argues that such ethical ideology does not enable us 'to name and strive for a Good', because it does little but to reinforce the divide between different political groups in society (Badiou 2002, 30). Such ethical ideology could be disrupted through dialogical nostalgia, as was indicated in the example of Jansen, who chose to forgive in an attempt to reconcile a situation. In doing so, he strove for Good as opposed to further fragmenting societal groups. Post-conflict societies working toward reconciliation ought to carefully consider the conception of ethics they adhere to since this inevitably trickles through societal discourses and often makes its way into the official curricula. Therefore, our conception of ethics can divide us and focus on what we share. In this sense, nostalgia becomes a useful construct to assist in formulating an ethic for post-conflict reconciliation.

One way to illustrate this ethical turn in the study of curriculum is in terms of intersectionality. This suggests the examination of social and cultural categories and the complex ethical relations between categories such as class, ethnicity, gender, race, religion and so on (Knudsen 2005). Applied to curriculum, it suggests researching spaces of intersection where we can begin to understand competing voices and to come to some understanding of how we understand the narratives of others. These understandings and intersectionality – according to Schields (2008) – are essential for social change. This kind of social change is not enforced upon people, but results from the ethical responsibility that people have towards one another. As Kristeva (1998) argues, it is not enough to study the difference and the inequality revealed by intersectional spaces – we also need to engage in the act of dismantling the nucleus of difference and inequality that leads to a divided existence. This, she argues, cannot be done through aggressive action, but through artful, imaginary engagement. The pursuit of dismantling nostalgia is one such artful, imaginary attempt to unearth ways of understanding competing narratives in the curriculum to facilitate social change and ultimately bring about reconciliation.

The idea of the ethical turn and the suggestion of intersectionality as a paradigm could further be conceptualised in terms of Lather's (2006) discussion of paradigm proliferation in education research methodology. In her earlier works, she presents three paradigms of post-positivist research – i.e., understand, emancipate and deconstruct – and a fourth possible paradigm (unnamed), which might usefully be interpreted as intersectionality (Lather 2006). Drawing on this notion, the purposes of curriculum could be as follows: curriculum to understand, curriculum to emancipate, curriculum to deconstruct and curriculum to intersect. Ontologically, a curriculum to understand refers to curriculum as a social reality informed by the phenomenological realm, whereas a curriculum to emancipate perceives of curriculum as a changeable historical-political configuration, one consisting of a set of relations that need to be revealed and engaged with critically (Delanty and Strydom 2003). Curriculum to deconstruct refers to curriculum as a complex form of social discourse that can only be understood from a point within (Delanty and Strydom 2003). The idea of curriculum as intersection is marked by a nexus of intersectional spaces, where the aim is dismantling of the nucleus of difference and inequality that leads to a divided existence (Kristeva 1998).

A curriculum to intersect, as a fourth possible paradigm, could be understood on three levels. Firstly, it denotes post-positivist paradigmatic proliferation as a way of thinking about curriculum. This suggests that we approach research in curriculum from a variety of perspectives to obtain a detailed view and thus establish a base for effective curriculum development. Put differently, our research should take place at the intersections of paradigms to fully represent the complex nature of, and conversations that shape, curriculum theory. Secondly, a curriculum aimed at intersection assumes that complex intersections of categories such as class, ethnicity, gender, race, religion and so on should be reflected in the enacted (or lived) curriculum as well as in the research we conduct. Thirdly, on a more abstract level, a curriculum to intersect also refers to the intersection of the past, present and future in the curriculum.

Reflective, dialogical nostalgia and curriculum to intersect: implications for post-conflict societies

Social reconciliation and peacebuilding initiatives in post-conflict societies are often criticised for being elitist and oblivious to the complex transformation required in such societies (Kumar 1999; Pouligny 2005). The focus of these initiatives is too often technical and financial in nature and does not place enough emphasis on existing societal structures, such as a national school curriculum, to facilitate social reconciliation and peacebuilding (Kumar 1999; Pouligny 2005). In the remainder of this article, I will discuss the implications that nostalgia might have for curriculum theorising, particularly on the school-level curriculum, that aims to lead people to the intersections of understanding through dialogue. However, before I begin the discussion, I need to explain why a curriculum can take us to such intersections. My point of departure is that the curriculum is the most powerful and influential document in a country, with an exceptional potential to generate social transformation. This is because it enables a space where individuals can share autobiographies and study lived experiences in their full complexity (Pinar 2010, 177). Its potential to create a platform for individuals to not only, 'recall the past from the point of view of the present, but to re-experience the past so that the pool of memory enlarges' situates both nostalgia and curriculum in broader reconciliatory discourses (177).

The problem is that the curriculum often serves as a 'dumping ground' for complex issues in society. This was confirmed in a recent meta-study that analysed the theoretical contributions made in 511 PhD theses delivered in South Africa between 2005 and 2012 (Du Preez and Simmonds forthcoming). The assumption is that any social problem, HIV/AIDS for instance, must be addressed in the curriculum. The result is that social problems are often dealt with in a reductionist fashion – they are divorced from their context and stripped of the dynamics that perpetuate such problems. Attention is given to the symptoms rather than the roots of complex social issues in the curriculum. A diagnostic approach would be more helpful in that it creates opportunities to explore the complex intersections that constitute the issues. In other words, this approach deals with the normative nature of an issue through engaging with it on an ontological and epistemological level. I will argue that dialogical nostalgia is an example of a diagnostic approach that could address some of the root causes of social issues.

Dillon (2009) argues that when we develop a theory of curriculum, we need to address three categories of questions. Firstly, we need to ask questions about the *nature* of curriculum. These include the essence and character of the curriculum. Secondly, we need to ask questions about the *elements* that comprise the curriculum. These elements include the teachers, learners, aims, results, subject milieus and activities in the curriculum.

Thirdly, we need to ask questions about *how to think and act* curriculum. The last category thus constitutes the methodological questions about the curriculum. Next, how the notion of curriculum to intersect plays out in Dillon's (2009) three categories of questions will be explored, whilst reference will be made to reflective, dialogical nostalgia.

The nature *of nostalgia in the curriculum*

To begin addressing the question of how nostalgia could assist us in realising a curriculum to intersect, a case will be described that demonstrates much of the current classroom practice – especially in the South African context. Slattery (2006) argues that our curricula often perpetuate a linear conception of time, which tends to delay meaning and purpose. Delaying meaning and purpose could be related to the symptomatic approach in curriculum to address social issues. Slattery (2006) illustrates this by providing the example of a child asking a teacher why s/he should study algebra and the teacher who answers that 'you'll need it in the future'. He argues that it is ethically mandatory that we '… create meaningful connections in each present moment …' and do not postpone meaning to some static (linear) future (86). His assertions also signify that our curricula cannot be understood as isolated spaces, but ought to be understood as borderless spaces where the present moments (for example the school and the workplace) could be reconciled through acknowledging the intersectional nature of social reality. Slattery adopts Friederich Nietzsche's view that time is eternally recurrent – a journey toward becoming and not a search for static meaning.

We need to acknowledge the ethical nature of curriculum as complicated conversation (Cary 2007; Pinar 2010) as well as its political nature (Chisholm 2005). The ethical turn that has emerged in curriculum enables us to step back from the political concerns in curriculum and to place ethics at the centre of our concern (Cary 2007). Some might argue that the political nature of the curriculum cannot receive secondary attention (especially in the historic-political context of South Africa and other post-conflict societies). However, Jansen (2009) argues that although critical theory has assisted us to understand the political nature of curriculum, it has not adequately assisted us to engage in reconciliatory discourses in post-conflict societies. He argues that critical theory tends to divide society because it necessitates that proponents take sides (Jansen 2009). For this reason, he argues against discourses that 'Other' and that repudiate the narratives that constitute our knowing and being (Jansen 2011). Thus, to place ethics at the core necessitates that we increase our epistemological awareness and positioning through sharing autobiographical journeys, through, for example, dialogical nostalgia, in curriculum spaces. In doing so we can study the 'discourses that frame our knowing and the way we know Others' (Cary 2007, 138). Placing ethics at the centre of curriculum theorising allows for curriculum to become, 'a historical event, changing over time as we participate in it, engage in its study and act in response to it' (Pinar 2010, 177). It is important to note that this line of reasoning does not aim to create a utopian vision of what schools ought to be like, that is, places of peaceful sharing. In fact, Jansen (2009) argues that our schools are spaces of profound divisions in which people:

> do not come with one story about the past, a common understanding of the present, and a shared vision of the future. It is divided knowledges *within* the classroom that constitute the starting point for a post-conflict pedagogy. (258–259, emphasis in original)

The profound divide creates a space where we can begin to think and act in an attempt to arrive at intersections of competing narratives. In this regard, Walder (2010) argues that nostalgia elicits contradictory voices and recreates turbulence and fragmentation through dialogue. He adds:

> ... it is not enough simply to recall the past, and turn it into a personal narrative of anger or guilt: recalling involves coming to terms with the past in an ethical as well as heuristic sense; it is to connect what you remember with the memories of others ... (14)

What I think is important for curriculum theorising in South Africa and other post-conflict societies is that we do not conceive of curriculum as a battlefield for equality through restoring and reinventing history. Instead, we need to reflect on our differences and specificity so we can arrive at intersections of understanding one another in the context of our ethical responsibilities towards one another. Reflective, dialogical nostalgia is important here since it enables us to position ourselves epistemologically and to transcend the isolated spaces often associated with traditional curriculum theorising.

The elements *of curriculum*

The nature of curriculum described above assumes a specific role for the teacher and the learner. It necessitates that these role players (and other education stakeholders) acknowledge that they are 'carriers of troubled knowledge' (Jansen 2009, 258). It is important to reflect on our nostalgias – the memory-bearers of our knowledge – in an honest manner and face the contradictions these often present. This epistemological positioning will put us in, 'a stronger – and more intellectually honest – position to deal with the many contingencies, arguments and agendas' (Hepburn 2003, 244). The process of epistemological positioning necessitates a process of self-reflexivity 'about and within nostalgia' so as to open up negotiation between the present and the past and discover how it shapes the self in relation to others (Walder 2010, 9).

Apart from the specific disposition required by teachers and learners, there need to be a clear vision and a curriculum that aim to create spaces where intersections could be dealt with. The aim cannot be to address the symptom of a problem – it needs to dismantle the roots of a problem. For example, if we desire a more peaceful society, we cannot merely speak about problems that hinder social cohesion – we need to delve deeply to find the elements that initially created and now perpetuate the problem. Here, reflective, dialogical nostalgia is a useful means of making a curriculum seek intersections since it might assist us in recognising our mutual pain, dealing with the knowledge streams that filter our messages about the past and the future, dealing with the political language we are exposed to, dealing with the reasons for inequality (such as poverty) and, in essence, dealing with the wrongdoings of the past (cf. Jansen 2011).

If we argue for a curriculum to intersect, we cannot view subject areas as isolated spaces since this might create artificial boundaries that can hinder us from arriving at intersections. Arriving at intersections of competing narratives requires that we acknowledge the complexity of knowledge, both in terms of our own epistemological positioning and in terms of subject knowledge. Handling this complexity through nostalgia is metaphorically described by Walder (2010) as 'dealing with broken mirrors' (12). In terms of curriculum theorising, this reasoning is in line with Bernstein's (2009) notion of the integrated curriculum (which is not synonymous with curriculum to intersect) that focuses not only on teaching, but also on coming to understand the 'ways of knowing'. Understanding the ways of knowing requires that we carefully consider the teaching-learning milieu, or curriculum spaces, in which we reflect nostalgically.

How to think and act *nostalgia in the curriculum*

Reflective, dialogical nostalgia enables praxis (reflection and action) in that it demands *reflection* of multiple social realities to facilitate the *act* of arriving at intersections of understanding competing narratives. Although competing narratives could never be understood in their entirety, we can arrive at moments of understanding through interaction. These moments could render possibilities of working conceptually towards a peaceful existence through acknowledging our shared interests (longing) and recognising our differences and specificity (homes).

On a more practical level, dialogue becomes the vehicle to capture and express reflective nostalgia. Our nostalgias (however different) can become the stimulus for dialogue (Du Preez 2008). The stimulus for dialogue – that is, nostalgia – might elicit immediate responses in terms of our shared longing and our divided homes, but it also has sufficient subtlety to spur ongoing thought (Jansen 2011). When our narratives and our nostalgias are 'desilenced' through dialogue, we are able to disrupt our ways of knowing and to begin finding intersections of understanding.

In sum, dialogical nostalgia can assist us in: dealing with matters of identity and trauma, rewriting bitter histories, historising the present and idealising the future (Walder 2010). In so doing, reflection can be translated into interaction and reflection that could bring competing narratives to intersecting spaces where understanding and action are possible. However, in this pursuit, Walder (2010) warns us about the fine line between sentimentality or melancholy, and critique or release, and that we should always be aware of the politics of representability when fragments of history are dealt with through nostalgia.

Conclusion

In this article, dialogical nostalgia was described in an attempt to steer curriculum theorising in a direction where it could allow for competing narratives to intersect, especially through the enacted school curriculum in post-conflict societies. It was argued that this is imperative to diagnostically deal with social issues that might influence reconciliation. In addition, dialogical nostalgia was positioned as an ethical imperative that is central to reconciliatory discourses. On a practical level, it was argued that dialogue is the vehicle of nostalgia and essential in the pursuit of desilencing complex voices about the past. The need for teachers and students to epistemologically position themselves was discussed, as well as the importance of an education vision that prioritises the need to deal with the past.

This attempt at rethinking curriculum theorising to desilence competing narratives and bringing curriculum as complicated conversation into fruition, focused mostly on how the past, present and future could become important for reconciliatory discourses. What requires more research is how paradigmatic proliferation – as an element of a curriculum to intersect – could assist in this pursuit. Qualitative research, especially drawing on narrative inquiry, would also be valuable in exploring the use of dialogical nostalgia.

In conclusion, in the same way that curriculum theory should evolve to respond to the changing social needs of a society, so too should our attempts to find ways to arrive at the intersections of competing voices evolve. This evolving nature is a prerequisite for reconciliation in post-conflict societies, which is also not static and secured. This evolutionary nature is an ethical imperative that requires thorough contemplation if reconciliation is to be taken seriously.

Notes
1. 'Narrative' in this article is used in a broad context to denote people's lived experiences; their life stories and social realities. The notion of 'typified

narratives' is used to illustrate that there are dominant discourses or clusters of narratives that represent a variety of individual narratives and that illustrate various political, cultural and historical beliefs and values. These typified narratives each contain specific symbols, myths and metaphors and could be understood as 'dominant evocations' (Soudien 2010, 1). When two or more of these typified narratives are in conflict, the notion of 'competing narratives' is used.
2. More about the history of nostalgia could be obtained from the work of Boym (2001).
3. At the time that this paper was first written and presented he was still the youth leader of the African National Congress. He has since been suspended from the party for a five-year period after being accused of corruption, sowing division within the ANC, and bringing the party into disrepute (Commey 2011a, 2011b).

References

Badiou, A. 2002. *Ethics: An Essay on the Understanding of Evil*. London: Verso.

Bernstein, B. 2009. "On the Curriculum." In *Curriculum. Organizing Knowledge for the Classroom*, edited by U. Hoadley and J. Jansen, 2nd ed., 287–291. Cape Town, South Africa: Oxford University Press.

Booth, K. 1999. "Three Tyrannies." In *Human Rights in Global Politics*, edited by T. Dunne and N. J. Wheeler, 31–70. Cambridge: Cambridge University Press.

Boym, S. 2001. *The Future of Nostalgia*. New York: Basic Books.

Cary, L. 2007. *Curriculum Spaces: Discourse, Postmodern Theory and Educational Research*. New York: Peter Lang.

Chisholm, L. 2005. "The Making of South Africa's *National Curriculum Statement*." *Journal of Curriculum Studies* 37 (2): 193–208.

Commey, P. 2011a. "The Malema Dilemma." *New African* (Nov): 18–22.

Commey, P. 2011b. "Malema Down and Out?" *New African* (Dec): 74–75.

Davis, F. 1979. *Yearning for Yesterday: A Sociology of Nostalgia*. London: Collier Macmillan.

Delanty, G., and P. Strydom. 2003. *Philosophies of Social Science. The Classic and Contemporary Readings*. Maidenhead: Open University Press.

Dillon, J. T. 2009. "The Questions of Curriculum." *Journal of Curriculum Studies* 41 (3): 343–359.

Dlamini, J. 2010. *Native Nostalgia*. Johannesburg, South Africa: Jacana Media.

Du Preez, P. 2008. "Dialogue as Facilitation Strategy: Infusing the Classroom with a Culture of Human Rights." PhD Diss, University of Stellenbosch, South Africa.

Du Preez, P., and S. Simmonds. Forthcoming. "Curriculum, Curriculum Development, Curriculum Studies? Problematising Theoretical Ambiguities in Doctoral Theses in the Education Field." *South African Journal of Education*.

Fairbanks, E. 2010. "The Healer. Can Jonathan Jansen Succeed Where Mandela Failed?" *The New Republic* (June 24): 15–19.

Gillespie, S. 2001. "Badiou's *Ethics*." *Pli* 12: 256–265.

Harper, R. 1966. *Nostalgia: An Existential Exploration of Longing and Fulfilment in the Modern Age*. Cleveland, OH: The press of Western Reserve University.

Hepburn, A. 2003. "Relativism and Feminist Psychology." In *Social Construction. A Reader*, edited by M. Gergen and G. Kenneth, 237–247. London: Sage.

Jansen, J. 2009. *Knowledge in the Blood*. Stanford, CA: Stanford University Press.

Jansen, J. 2011. *We Need to Talk*. Northlands, South Africa: Macmillan.
Knudsen, S. V. 2005. "Intersectionality – A Theoretical Inspiration in the Analysis of Minority Cultures and Identities in Textbooks." Paper presented at the eighth international conference on Learning and Educational Media, Caen, October.
Kristeva, J. 1998. "Women's Time." In *Continental Philosophy: An Anthology*, edited by W. McNeill and K. Feldman, 406–415. Malden, MA: Blackwell.
Kumar, K. 1999. *Promoting Social Reconciliation in Postconflict Societies. Selected Lessons from USAID's Experience*. Washington, DC: Centre for Development Information and Evaluation, US Agency for International Development.
Lather, P. 2006. "Paradigm Proliferation as a Good Thing to Think with: Teaching Research in Education as a Wild Profusion." *International Journal of Qualitative Studies in Education* 19 (1): 35–57.
Marais, W., and J. C. De Wet. 2009. "The Reitz Video: Inviting Outrage and/or Pity?" *Communitas* 14 (1): 27–42.
Margalit, A. 2002. *The Ethics of Memory*. Cambridge, MA: Harvard University Press.
McLeod, J., and R. Thomson. 2009. *Researching Social Change*. London: Sage.
Morrison, K. 2004. "The Poverty of Curriculum Theory: A Critique of Wraga and Hlebowitsh." *Journal of Curriculum Studies* 36 (4): 487–494.
Pinar, W. 2009. "The Reconceptualization of Curriculum Studies." In *The Curriculum Studies Reader*, edited by D. J. Flinders and S. J. Thornton, 168–175. New York: Taylor & Francis.
Pinar, W. 2010. "Currere." In *Encyclopedia of Curriculum Studies*, edited by C. Kridel, 176–177. London: Sage.
Pinar, W. 2011. "Allegories-of-the-Present: Curriculum Design in a Culture of Narcissism and Presentism." Paper presented at the first international conference on Curriculum and Instruction, Eskisehir, Turkey, October.
Pouligny, B. 2005. "Civil Society and Post-Conflict Peacebuilding: Ambiguities of International Programmes Aimed at Building 'New' Societies." *Security Dialogue* 36 (4): 495–510.
Schields, S. A. 2008. "Gender: An Intersectionality Perspective." *Sex Roles* 59 (5–6): 301–311.
Slattery, P. 2006. *Curriculum Development in the Postmodern Era*. 2nd ed. New York: Routledge.
Soudien, C. 2010. "Who Takes Responsibility for the 'Reitz Four'? Puzzling Our Way through Higher Education Transformation in South Africa." *South African Journal of Science* 106 (9/10): 1–4.
Walder, D. 2010. *Postcolonial Nostalgias: Writing, Representation, and Memory*. New York: Routledge.

Index

abolition of apartheid 7, 117–18, 123
acting curricular nostalgia 132–3
activism 71, 81, 103–5
addressing intercultural conflict 77–9
affective engagement 60–62
Affouneh, S. 18, 34
agents for positive change 24, 33–6
aims of global citizenship 59–60
Akar, B. 17
Al Azhar mosque 45, 47
altering values 34; *see also* awareness-raising; Freire, Paulo
Alyan, Hala 104
ambiguity 11, 25–6
American University of Beirut 97–100, 102, 104; *see also* youth narratives
amnesia 6–7
Andersson, L. 19
Andreotti, V. 61, 71
animosity 2
anti-Islam 80; *see also* Islam
apartheid 7, 117–18, 123
Apple, M. W. 19
approaches to dialogue 81–2
approaches to diversity 79–80
Arab Spring 1, 107
Arab world 32–52; *see also* teaching for forgiveness
Arafat, Yasser 44–5, 47
Ardizzone, L. 15
ARROW programme *see* Art: a Resource for Reconciliation Over the World
Art: a Resource for Reconciliation Over the World 6, 77–96
articulating injustice 77–96; arts as non-verbal dialogue 87–91; conclusion 93–5; contested approaches to dialogue 81–2; contested approaches to diversity 79–80; critical dialogue through storytelling 91–3; diversity and conflict 84–5; drawing on arts 82–4; illustrating the data 85–7; introduction 77–9

arts as form of dialogue 77–96
arts-based critical dialogue 91–3
arts-based transformative dialogue 85–7
attempting to teach for forgiveness 38–9
attitudes to diversity 63–5
attitudes to global citizenship 71
attitudes towards forgiveness 32–3
Au, W. 19
AUB *see* American University of Beirut
awareness-raising 34

backstage behaviour 110
Badiou, A. 127
Bajaj, M. 19
Bakhtin, M. 24
'banking' education 24, 72, 78
Bartolome, L. 23
Beirut Spring 104, 107–8
Bekerman, Z. 17
beliefs about forgiveness 32–3
Bernstein, B. 132
between memory and history 122
beyond cessation of violence 53–6
Bickmore, K. 65
Boal, Augusto 84
Booth, K. 123
Boulding, E. 33, 48
Boym, Svetlana 118–19, 122–5
'broken mirrors' 132
'broken society' 77–8
brutalisation 2
Buber, M. 24
Burbules, N. C. 24, 84
Burnett, J. 80

Cairns, E. 14
Cameron, David 77–8
'Can the Subaltern Speak?' 81, 83
Cantle, E. 80
carriers of troubled knowledge 131
Cary, L. 127

INDEX

categorisation 65, 72–3
Catholicism 53–76
celebration of difference 88–9, 94
cessation of violence 53–6
challenges of humanising education 7–8
challenges to global citizenship 69–70
character education 32–3
Christianity 35, 38, 41–2, 49
chronos 120–22
citizenship education 16–17
civic responsibilities 16–17
Coles, R. 18
collaboration 66–8, 72
collective memory 2, 6–7, 20–21, 122
colonialism 81
comfort zone 101
commitment 2
communicative action 91
Community Cohesion strategy 80
compassion 2–3, 23, 35
competing intersecting narratives 133
complement to dialogue 93–5
comprehensive peace education 53
concept of 'banking' 24, 72, 78
concept of critical reflection 71
concept of peacebuilding 11–12
conflict in SW England 84–5
conflict transformation programme 77–96
conflict-sensitive education 13
'conscientization' 34, 81; *see also* awareness-raising; Freire, Paulo
constraints on critical dialogic discourse 53–76
consumerism 71, 111–12
consumption of cultural difference 61
contact zone 101
contested approaches to dialogue 81–2
contested approaches to diversity 79–80
contextual features of Arab education 36–7
cosmopolitanism 60
creative re-storying 21
creative writing workshops 100–113; activism 103–5; disillusionment 105–113; idealism 102–3
critical dialogic discourse in schools 53–76
critical dialogue 91–3
critical education 19–20
critical reflection principles 56–7, 62, 70–73
culturalism 123
culture of peace 21–2, 48
culture of silence 83
curricular nostalgia 132–3
curriculum to intersect 117–35

data triangulation 57–9
Davies, L. 55, 62

Davis, Fred 118
deconstruction 54
dehumanisation 14, 23
Delanty, G. 54
Denham, S. 48
deprivation of rights 14, 23
desensitisation 98–100
desilenced nostalgia 132–3
development of critical dialogic discourse 53–76
Dewey, J. 19, 23
dialogic humanisation 22–5; dialogue as humanising pedagogy 23–5; humanising force of education 22–3
dialogic nostalgia 126, 129–33; *see also* nostalgia
dialogic pedagogy 1–9, 46, 54
dialogical nostalgia 117–35
dialogue as humanising pedagogy 22–5
difference 117–18
differences between school attitudes 65–9
Dillon, J. T. 129–30
disengagement 107
disharmony 2
disillusionment 105–114
diversity 3, 84–5; in SW England 84–5
divided society 10–11, 53–76
Dlamini, Jacob 118–19, 121, 123, 125–6
domestication education 78
drawing on arts as dialogue 82–4
Duggan, D. 83, 86
Dunlap, R. E. 71
Dupuy, K. 15
dysfunction 104

eagerness to teach for forgiveness 45–9
economic dispossession 81
economic redistribution 53–4, 71
education as humanisation 22–3
education for peacebuilding *see* peacebuilding education
education system in Arab world 36–7
elements of curriculum 131–2
elevation of similarity 88–9, 94
emancipation 22–4
embracing ethical turn 126–8
emergency education 13
emotional engagement 55, 71–2
empathy 21
engagement 55, 60–62, 71–2, 90–91
England 84–5
enthusiasm for teaching global issues 59–69; aims of global citizenship 59–60; attitudes to diversity 63–5; school approaches/difference 65–9; understandings of interdependence 60–62

INDEX

environmental awareness 60–62, 71
equity 16
ethical turn in curriculum 126–8
Eurocentrism 61
exploitation 84
exploration of youth experience of participation 77–96
exploring nostalgia 118–26; from doctors to poets/philosophers 119–20; irony through space and time 120–22; silent, dialogic nostalgia 122–6; in the twilight zone 122

facilitating data triangulation 57–9
Fair Trade 62
Fairbanks, E. 123–4
Faour, M. 36, 46
fear 2, 18
figures of forgiveness 43–5
fluidity 113–14
forgiveness pedagogy 40–41
forgiveness, teaching for 5, 32–53; *see also* reconciliation
formal curriculum content 39–40
fostering respect 21–2
Frankfurt School of Sociology 19
Fraser, N. 53
Freire, Paulo 3, 10–11, 19–25, 34, 46, 54–7, 64–72, 78–82, 92
from doctors to poets 119–20; *see also* nostalgia; reconciliation
frontstage behaviour 110
Future of Nostalgia 118

Gadamer, H.-G. 3, 81, 92
Gallagher, T. 66–8, 79–80, 88, 94
Galtung, J. 11–13, 22
Gandin, L. A. 19
Gill, Scherto 8
Giroux, F. 34, 55, 62, 72
global citizenship 53–76; conclusion 70–73; context 57; implementation of 69–70; introduction 53–6; research methods 57–9; results 59–69; theoretical framework 56–7
Global South 25, 65
Goffman, Erving 109–110
Good Friday Agreement 57
Green, R. 80, 89
group stereotyping 2, 33

Habermas, Jürgen 81–2, 92–3
Hage, Ghassan 109
Hammett, D. 60
Hariri, Rafic 98, 103–4, 113
harmony 42
Harper, Ralph 118
'having fun' 100, 109–110

hedonism 99
hermeneutical approaches 19
Hinge, H. 19
Hirsch, Marianne 99
history education 20–21
HIV/AIDS 129
Hofer, Johannes 119
holistic understanding of peacebuilding 12, 18
hope of the future 113–14
hopelessness 18
horizon of understanding 81, 94
horizontal collaboration 3
human dignity 21–2
humanisation 63–5, 71–2
humanising pedagogy 22–5
humans-in-relationship 78
hüzün 105; *see also* melancholy
hypothetical forgiveness scenarios 37–8

ideal of dialogue 81
idealism 102–3
identity deconstruction 54
identity-based conflict 57
illustrating data 85–7
implementing global citizenship 69–70
implications for post-conflict societies 129–33
in the twilight zone 122
individual ontological vocation 3
inexpressibility of pain 100
injustice 77–96
insecurities 113–14
institutionalised racism 85, 95
insularity 59
intense lived experiences 97–9
intercultural conflict 77–9
interdependence 60–62
intergroup forgiveness 35, 59
internal cognitive transformation 54
intersectionality 126–33
intifada 98–9, 104–6
intra-community conflict 35–6
irony 118–22
Islam 35, 38–49, 80
isolation 23
Istanbul: Memories of a City 105

Jansen, Jonathan 118, 125, 127, 131
Janus face of education 25
Jenkins, T. 15
Judaism 35

kairos 120–22
Keet, A. 23
Kegels, Nicolien 99–100
Kent, G. 34
Khalaf, Samir 109, 111

INDEX

Korostelina, K. 13
Kristeva, J. 128

lack of articulation 60
language 23–5
'Language of Nostalgia' 126
Larkin, Craig 99
Lebanese Civil War 98, 102
Lebanon 97–116; *see also* youth narratives
Lebanon Adrift 109, 111
Lederach, J.-P. 11–13, 78, 82–4, 91–2, 94
Ledwith, Margaret 91
Leitch, Ruth 82–3, 90, 94
Liebmann, Marian 91
linear understanding of time 120–22; *see also* nostalgia; reconciliation
literature review 99–100
lived experiences 97–9
living peacefully together 10–11, 23

McInnis, D. 13
McLeod, J. 121
McMurray, A. 62
Mahdavi, Pardis, 100, 111
Maiese, M. 12
Malema, Julius 124–5
Margalit, A. 122
marginalisation 91
Matarasso, François 82, 92
MDGs *see* Millennium Development Goals
melancholy 105, 119–20
memory fatigue 122
Messina, C. 19
Middle East *see* Arab world
Millennium Development Goals 10–11
Mitchell, G. 12
Moeschberger, S. L. 35
moral global citizenship 55–6
Moral Imagination 83
morality 72
Morrison, K. 127
motivation to forgive 41–3
multiculturalism 79–80, 94

narcissistic excess 113–14
narrative maze 100
narratives of difference 90–91, 117–18
national imaginary 80, 128
Native Nostalgia 118
nature of nostalgia 130–31
need for theoretical development 4–7
need to teach for forgiveness 5, 38–9
needs of young people 36
negative peace 11, 14
Netherlands 55–7, 66
Niens, U. 62

Nietzsche, Friederich 130
9/11 *see* September 11
non-verbal dialogue 83–4, 87–91; *see also* arts as form of dialogue
Northern Ireland 35, 53–76, 83; *see also* global citizenship
nostalgia 117–35
notion of humanisation 2–4
Nussbaum, M. C. 54, 56

objective truth 21
obsessive compulsive disorder 119–20
OCD *see* obsessive compulsive disorder
Oddie, David 78–9
one-dimensional understanding of space 120–22; *see also* nostalgia; reconciliation
open global citizenship 55–6
opportunities of humanising education 7–8
optimism 103
'Other' 2–3, 17, 20–21, 33–4, 54, 88–9, 94, 130
outrage 55
overcoming isolation 23

Painted Reflections 104
painting the picture 84–5
Pamuk, Orhan 105
Papastephanou, M. 35
Parekh, B. 71
participation 77–96
peacebuilding education 10–31, 53–76
peacekeeping 11
peacemaking 11
pedagogical approaches to peacebuilding education 15–22; citizen education 16–17; critical education 19–20; fostering respect 21–2; history education 20–21; values education 17–19
pedagogy of forgiveness 40–41
pedagogy of the oppressed 19, 22
Pedagogy of the Oppressed 81
pedagogy for peacebuilding education 25–6
perceptions of forgiveness 41–3
peripheral attitudes 25
pillars of learning 13
Pinar, W. 127
Pinto, R. 80, 89
plurality of values 18
Porteus, K. 23
positive peace 11, 14
post-conflict peacebuilding 1–9
post-conflict societies 117–35
post-memory generation 97–9
post-modern hybridity 103
post-war landscape 97–116; *see also* youth narratives
Postcolonial Nostalgias 118–19

INDEX

Postmemory 99
potential variation in attitudes 72–3
power imbalances 23–4
principles of critical reflection 56–7, 70–73; reflecting Freirean concepts 71; role of emotional engagement 71–2; Veugelers' categorisation 72–3
Pritchard, R. 79–80, 88, 94
promoting MDGs 10–11
Protestantism 53–76
pupil attitudes to global citizenship 71–2

qualitative analysis themes 38–45; forgiveness figures/symbols 43–5; forgiveness in formal curriculum 39–40; forgiveness pedagogy 40–41; motivation to forgive 41–3; need to teach for forgiveness 38–9
qualitative survey data 57–9
Quaynor, L. 17
Queen's University Belfast 58

racial discrimination 77, 80, 85, 123
racial segregation 88–9, 117–18
re-imagined relationships 12
Reardon, B. A. 53–4
rebuilding relationships 78
recall of emotions 119–20; *see also* nostalgia; reconciliation
reconciliation 3–5, 21–2, 34, 68–9, 117–35; conclusion 133; embracing ethical turn 126–8; exploring nostalgia 118–26; narratives of difference 117–18; reflective, dialogical nostalgia 129–33
reconstruction of community relationships 1–9; conclusion 7–8; need for theoretical development 4–7; notion of humanisation 2–4
reducing stereotyping 33, 89
reflective nostalgia 129–33; acting nostalgia 132–3; elements of curriculum 131–2; nature of nostalgia 130–31
Reitz event 123–5
religion 35
religious discourse 45–9
repression 14, 19
research participants 38
respect 21–2
responsible global citizenship 53–5
restorative nostalgia 123–6
retaliation 34–5
retribalisation 106
review of dialogic pedagogy role 10–31
review of Lebanese literature 99–100
rioting 77–9, 91
role of dialogic pedagogy 10–31; conclusion 25–6; dialogic humanising pedagogy 22–5; introduction 10–11; peacebuilding as transformative process 11–12; pedagogical approaches to peacebuilding education 15–22; role of education in peacebuilding 12–15
role of education 12–15
role models 18, 38–46, 48
Roman, L. G. 61
root causes of violent conflict 11–12, 14, 24–6

safe expression 83
safety net 101
Said, Edward 103
Salomon, G. 14, 24–5
Schields, S. A. 128
school approaches 65–9
school development of critical dialogic discourse 53–76
sectarian violence 97–8
self-confidence 37
self-esteem 33
self-reflexivity 131–2
self-reporting 56
semi-structured interviews 37–8; participants 38
September 11 1, 79–80
sexual abuse 14
sexual boundaries 110
Shapiro, S. 23, 54
shared memory *see* collective memory
Shultz, L. 73
silent nostalgia 122–6, 132–3
Slattery, P. 117, 130
Sleeping Beauty 118
Smith, A. 13–15, 17
Snauwaert, D. T. 53
Social Impact of Participation in the Arts 82
social media 39
social segregation 57
societal transformation 12–15, 34, 54–6, 62
Soudien, C. 124
South Africa 117–35
Spivak, Gayatri, 81
Staeheli, L. A. 60
static truth 21
stereotyping 2, 33, 78, 88–90, 94
storytelling 82–3, 90–93
structural constraints on discourse 53–76
sustainable peace 11
symbols of forgiveness 43–5
systems of Arab education 36–7

Taif Accord 1990 98, 102
teacher conceptualisations of global citizenship 71–2
teaching for forgiveness 32–52; Arab education systems 36–7; implications 45–9; introduction

INDEX

32–3; methods and techniques 37–8; results 38–45; theoretical framework 33–6
Theatre of the Oppressed 84
theory of conflict transformation 91
theory of democratic education 19
thinking curricular nostalgia 132–3
Thompson, P. 24
Thomson, R. 121
tolerance 13
towards conflict transformation 85–7
trans-generational transmission of trauma 13–14
transcending inequality 54
transformative processes 11–12, 54
Transit Beirut 103
trauma 2, 13–14, 20–22, 82–3, 98
trends in global citizenship 69–70
twilight zone 122
Twitter 124–5

unconditional mercy 35
understanding global citizenship 71
understandings of interdependence 60–62
UNESCO 13, 18
UNICEF 12–14
unifying identity 54
urf 48–9
utilising arts 77–96

values education 17–19
Van Liere, K. D. 71
Vaux, T. 13–14
Veugelers, W. 55–7, 65–6, 72–3
violence 117–18
Vriens, L. 14

Walder, Dennis 118–19, 122, 131–3
war on terror 80
Watkins, K. 36
We Need to Talk 118
Wegerif, R. 3
Western trends 39, 55
Winter, C. 71
Worley, C. 80
wrongdoing 33, 47

Yearning for Yesterday 118
youth experience of participation 77–96
youth narratives 97–116; conclusion 113–14; introduction 97–9; literature review 99–100; methodology and content 100–113
Youthful Voices in Post-war Lebanon 98–9

Zembylas, M. 17
Zinn, D. 23